CONSIDER THIS

On Stage Being The Pastor's Younger First Lady

A Memoir

EXPERIENCED BY

Amy J Lee-Coleman

CONSIDER THIS ON STAGE BEING THE PASTOR'S YOUNGER FIRST LADY

iUniverse books may be ordered through booksellers or by contacting:

iUniverse
1663 Liberty Drive
Bloomington, IN 47403
www.iuniverse.com
844-349-9409

"All Scripture used is the American Standard Version unless otherwise noted."

ISBN: 978-1-6632-1530-7 (sc)
ISBN: 978-1-6632-1531-4 (e)

Library of Congress Control Number: 2020925362

Print information available on the last page.

iUniverse rev. date: 02/19/2021

Dedicated to the two along for the ride …

To my beloved daughter, *Mookii*, I pray you understand now that this overall journey was ordained by God just for me. Thanks for allowing your mother to listen to God and follow her heart! I pray you have learned to listen to God with your heart and know that I so respect the young woman you have become. My love for you is eternal!

To my husband of many years, Pastor Emeritus James E. Coleman, my honey pastor, it is because of you and our life together that this book is possible. Thank you for loving us and for these stages of life that allowed me to grow, which gave me a testimony to share. As your first lady, I was thrust upon a stage like none other when I said, "I do." That stage was and is challenging, but I've learned to lean and depend on God the Father forevermore. Much love and respect, my prince!

My sincere prayer is that my journey blesses someone to truly understand what God will do in your marriage if you are ever placed in a challenging position (such as becoming the first lady of a church on top of being much younger than your husband). This book was written for my sanity and clarity. I learned that the expectations of people can never be met. Just consider that there are life lessons to be learned, so pay close attention and get yours.

So that they are no more two, but one flesh. What therefore

God hath joined together, let not man put asunder.

Matthew 19:6

Consider This

Having a relationship with Your Father means you can stay in His care always and be who He created you to be for His glory.

THEMES OF MY STAGE EXPERIENCES

Before the Stage

I was a single, divorced mother of a happy eleven-year-old little girl whose upbringing was my main focus. I also had a career and was working in ministry to bless God's people through missions. Yes, I was ***alone but never lonely yet somehow not whole.***

Stage 1

A good friend introduced me to a longtime family friend of hers and her late father's. After we met, in my mind, I was thinking, *What is wrong with me?* because something inside of me was interested. **There was a twenty-six-year age difference, and he was a minister (former pastor)? Not in this lifetime!**

Stage 2

It just goes to show once again that you never know what God is doing because **the reverend was chasing, and I was running, but God was working it out for my good.**

Stage 3

So I surrendered and we begin to date. But a few people who had doubts about us being together because of the age difference, and **they said, "Don't do it." (Was it Christian love or messy church folks?)** Only God could and would reveal that truth in His time.   11

Stage 4

I realized that at some point I had to start to believe what God had said in all the messages He sent to me. Pay attention because He answers and guides you in the way you should go, and He does not make mistakes. So we began **preparing for "I do," focusing on God, *not* outside negative interference.**   16

Stage 5

So after God confirmed what was to be, we married, and all was well with us even in spite of others' disbelief. I knew in my spirit that he was meant to be a pastor; it was in the way he carried himself. And as God would have it, he became a pastor again! That was when I began to have doubts in some areas as well, asking myself, **"Did he really take *me* as his wife?" (Was I a showpiece as the first lady or a helpmeet?)**   20

Stage 6

I slowly came to realize that our age difference would make a difference in how I would be as the first lady of any church. He did make it clear to the church that he loved me. However, there was never any clear perception of what he wanted my role to be in the church, and that opened the door to all kinds of treatment for this first lady. At any rate, lesson learned: turn inward to God, and He will get you through it all. So God led me to begin focusing on my relationship with my husband and **becoming the right person for my husband. (It was *never* about me!)**   26

Stage 7

Not only would I walk into a new role as first lady but we had to include my old role of first being a mother to my one and only child. She had her own perceptions. All his children were grown and gone. **Add a twelve-year-old to the equation. Inclusion in blending required much attention and time**, but with God, all is possible.   31

Stage 8

Even though my focus became about us as man and wife, I still had to attend church before God's people. So whether I understood it or not or even accepted it, the title was given. **What does the term *first lady* mean to me and for us?**   36

Stage 9

I came from a church where service in ministry was normal and consistent. The mission field was real and thriving throughout each year, and I loved it. As an adult, service to others was already a lifestyle for me. God showed me that was part of my purpose, and I lived it daily, **ministry in action. Oh, but not so fast, new first lady!**   46

Stage 10

Serving in the mission field was a way of life for me as we dated. Even after we married, there were overnight mission trips, and it seemed he was elated about my being active in service, but something was different. *What changed—a husband's covering or a pastor's wife left to fend for herself?*

Stage 11

Even though God had me walk through many trials that still exist, I learned to navigate them better by *staying focused on God's Will for us with His help.* Were we **servants for God or serving others' expectations?** So now I turn to God in fervent prayer for any and all situations that may come my way and never let it be about others.

Stage 12

True pastors are called—we know that. A divine call to God's service is a biblical vocation. Surrendering and committing to that full-time takes the grace of God every step of the way. However, the pastor's wife must see to it that the family has its time as well. We must remember that God sent the wife to help her husband. There has to be balance for the man of God. **Family time without the church is a must-have!**

Stage 13

We have to be realistic and understand that there is no written plan for pastors to exit the pulpit. Either they retire when age or illness becomes an issue, or God in His majesty calls them home to glory. *When the pulpit is behind the pastor* after forty plus years of service, Lord Jesus, now what?

Stage 14

I came to realize that we can face any and all struggles with confidence and assurance in God's care. He cannot fail, for He is not a man. Relying on God is the best and only way to get through every situation in life. We can rest in confidence. ***Calmness is here because God's got us in and through it all.***

And so it begins …

Taking the walk to the stage and stepping into the different world of First Ladydom!

BEFORE THE STAGE

Alone but Never Lonely yet Somehow Not Whole

The word *alone* means having no one present or being on one's own. The word *lonely* means being sad because one has no friends or company. I have been alone many times, but never have I been lonely for long periods. In my opinion, being alone is a choice, and loneliness is only temporary. Wallowing in being alone can often make one desperate for attention and lead one into unhealthy relationships. Women, does the word *thirsty* come to mind? I have always been fortunate enough to recognize the difference between the two and knew that being single or alone was not for me. As an adult of a certain age, I was never meant to be alone, and I knew that fact early on in life. Knowing that God created woman for man and that the two should become one and procreate to make a family, I understood that but did not really understand that God had to send my mate. Therefore, submitting was a learned process, as I am sure it is for everyone who loves the Lord and wants to live for Him. So I tried some things—some dumb things—on my own. You know, as young women, we see a man, and we want him, or we think we want him, because we are only looking at the outer part of a man. So my understanding of God sending my mate came much later.

Being in a single-parent home, I was made to attend church to hear the Word of God and to be active in ministry. From that perspective, there was no doubt I was made to understand right from wrong at a young age. There were things you just did not do. It was instilled in me so well that even if I did do something wrong, I felt so bad about it that I would tell on myself. I did not like my momma being upset or disappointed in me. I knew how hard she worked, so I did not want to make her life any harder than it was already. Plus, if you grow up in a household where someone is always getting into trouble, seeing that behavior can help tremendously in showing you what not to do to upset your parent. I saw that, and I tried real hard, even to a fault, to stay out of trouble.

Although I grew up in a single-family home, I was exposed to family life with a mother and a father by spending time with my relatives who had an only child. Even though no father figure was in my home as I was growing up, in that family, I saw what it was like to have both parents at home. Being with them was like having a father and second mother. My second mother was there when my momma couldn't be. I spent many weekends with them and yearly vacations too. I never saw them have a cross word with each other. Understanding relationships as I do now, I am sure they did have arguments, but they did not argue in front of us. What I saw was them kissing, touching, and holding each other in front me and their child. I saw them cherish each other and have good times together along with family and friends on a regular basis.

I also grew up with a great work ethic. They, along with my momma, showed us by example how working hard for your family allowed you to live well, enjoy life, have fun, and give back. Although I never really saw my mother play hard, my relatives not only worked hard but they played hard as well. They all were examples of helping others by supporting those in need. So I saw balance, which was a great preparation for being an adult. A loving family home was not foreign to me at all. I saw love in both homes. It appeared in different ways, but it was there. I not only saw it but I felt it too. I was loved by both.

The idea of being married was always appealing to me. I knew that God intended for two to become one. Now, watching my mother, I saw she had a different take on relationships. She seemed to make the choice to be alone and became satisfied with being by herself. It was obvious that her children were her life. And that was okay for her because we all have choices we have to make for our lives. I realized that did not have to be my choice. I became open to what my life would be like if I shared it with someone special. Because I had seen a loving couple in a home, I knew someday I wanted the same thing. I was meant to be married and assumed that there would be someone who thought the same way as I did.

I also learned at an early age that misery is an option. One does not have to be miserable. For the Word of God in Philippians 4:11, to paraphrase tells us that *we can learn to be content whatever the circumstance and in any and all situations.* Sometimes, we create or buy into misery for ourselves by making bad decisions. I learned we have choices in all situations and how we deal with them, whether good or bad. Joshua 24:15a, c says, "And if it seem evil unto you to serve Jehovah, *choose* you this day whom ye will serve; but as for me and my house, we will serve Jehovah." The choice or the free will that God gives is a beautiful thing, and it's always available. The old folks used to say, "Serving the Lord will pay off," and it will every single time. I had to learn to recognize that more often and to take it more seriously. Again, there are choices, and I can make them for myself with God's help.

I believe while surrendering to do good, there will still be a fight against bad, which requires much help from God. That helps in realizing the fight is against evil and not me. Sometimes, things will not go well. The acceptance of that fact helps also.

Thinking I knew what was required of me as a wife, I married after ten years of dating. Yes, ten years! I actually was in junior high school when we met, and there was a three-year age difference. He was older and in high school. It was my first love, and I thought we would be together forever. There was nothing like it, and it hit me like a ton of bricks. I was young and believed everything was right with our world and nothing could make me think differently about it. What I found was that I lost *me* in it. Only God could make this young, starry-eyed girl look inward and find herself again, but she had to go through some things to find her way back.

It seemed I was always attracted to older men, and older men were attracted to me. I have always been told that I seem older than I actually am or that I have an old soul. All I knew was that I did not like foolishness and did not want to play games with anyone, no matter his age. And that is what men my age or younger seem to be about, foolishness. Yes, I said *younger*. I tried that too. I was looking for a committed relationship with someone who wanted to be in it with me and only me. Truly, a give-and-take partnership with the good and bad is what I was looking for—something a couple could work on together while building a future. Again, I thought I was ready to give what was required in a real relationship. I had to allow God to open my eyes because, first of all, I should not have been looking and trying to find a life partner. The man is supposed to find his wife, right? As my honey pastor would say, the Bible says, "Whoso findeth a wife findeth a good thing, And obtaineth favor of Jehovah" Proverbs 18:22. And in his findings, he should be trying to please God, which brings him favor!

My first marriage lasted for ten years and was nothing like I thought it would be. Now, I did not expect it to be a fairy tale, but I did expect it to last. I went into it thinking that I had the tools needed for a lasting relationship but learned that one cannot do it alone and without God. So I messed up in some of my decisions, thinking I could fix what was broken. That did not work. One can only fix oneself—or make the effort to do so. When making the effort, it shows you realize you need work. I learned that whoever another person chooses to be, he or she will be, with or without a partner.

With the help of the Holy Spirit, the light bulb finally came on, and the time came for me to begin to work on myself in my situation. That was when my relationship began to shift because I was growing up and allowing God to make a change in me. Hello, lone-Lee-ness!

Actually, looking back, if I am honest, I did feel lonely at times. To tell the truth, a lot of those years I was really alone and never whole but not by choice. I just lost myself for a time, but now I realize I had to go through all that to learn valuable life lessons. So then, things began to change, which was supposed to happen. Now, I saw signs, but I overlooked them. Why? I was in the fix-it mode. We all will change, which should be a part of learning and growing for the better. But sometimes that change is for the worse, and we miss or ignore signs that are right in our faces, as I did. Again, we women tend to think we can fix a situation, so we allow things to go on and on.

People will show you who they are, but we see what we want to see and we think we can change them. I did because those early signs were saying maybe this was not right for me, but not listening to the Holy Spirit will get you what you don't need and a lot of heartache every time. Learning to look through God's eyes all the time and pay attention when the Holy Spirit shows you what is not right is the key. Do I fail sometimes? Yes, and I probably will continue to, but I am learning lessons!

Perfection is never the goal because it can't be attained in human form. It is being open to change sent my way and being ready to admit my flaws, not making excuses but realizing God can and will sustain me for what is ahead.

Consider This

Pay attention when God speaks, and act according to His will for each of *your* life circumstances.

STAGE 1

Twenty-Six-Year Age Difference and a Minister (Former Pastor)? Not in This Lifetime!

The Word of God states that "whoso findeth a wife findeth a good thing, And obtaineth favor of Jehovah" Proverbs 18:22. It does not mention age in the scriptures. Although the Bible does speak of age in Ruth 3 and 4 when Boaz agreed to marry a young woman named Ruth in order for her to keep land in her family because her husband was dead. That proved it was not about her age. It also says, "Therefore shall a man leave his father and his mother, and shall cleave unto his wife: and they shall be one flesh" Genesis 2:24. Again, there is no mention of age or vocation.

Marrying a man twenty-six years my elder after only knowing him for eight months was not in my plan; nor was marrying a pastor. But listening to God will get you what you think you don't want every time. Once you decide to live in His will for your life, He will send what is needed or is best for you and not what you think is best. You not gone get what you want! Remember, you are in His will when you ask for His will to be done in your life. Now, God does not lie and will give you the desires of your heart that are in His will if your trust is in him. We conveniently leave out that part of the scripture all the time. The Bible says, "Delight thyself also in the Jehovah: and he will give thee the desires of thy heart. Commit thy way unto the Jehovah; trust also in him; and he will bring it to pass" Psalm 37:4–5. Wow, was that made a reality in my personal life! I found out that I was not specific in all areas of what I asked God for, thus the age difference and his chosen vocation, which were minor compared to the major things I asked for and He supplied. He knows what we need. That's why we must be careful when asking God for anything.

When God answers, we don't see that it is best for us because our spiritual eyes are not always open. Let's just be honest about it: that's when we are in the "what I want" mode. The flesh is still very much alive when living for God. Daily, we have to fight temptations by including Him in all our decisions, which is the only way to resist. I read somewhere long ago where someone once called it "Spirit-filled resistance." So we should ask Him first. I believe now, looking back, that God was laughing at me because I was allowing my flesh to have a say and listening to those around me. I have heard many times over the years that God has a sense of humor. And, yes, you have to laugh sometimes to keep from crying. That is truly a way of getting through. I also know that crying can be very cleansing, and I have done my share of it. I truly understand that because leading up to the point of accepting what is best for you can be challenging and scary. So I did cry and still do sometimes. That is my way of releasing and getting it out of my system so I don't take it out on anyone. It seems to work best for me to be able to move on. That is another thing it is good to find out: what works for you with God's help.

The age difference, does it really matter in any relationship, especially marriage? Only if those involved make it an issue is what I believe. People, men and women, are basically the same no matter what—in terms of we are all, male and female, made by God to come together as man and wife with the purpose of reproducing. We forget that, but that is God's way. Age should not be a factor for the flesh if God has His hand in it. Mature people understand this to be true. People who have gone through some things realize it as well, and I am in that category. At any and all ages, marriage requires work and should be what you make it. If you make a commitment or promise, keep it. Yes, promises will be broken. That comes with the fleshly part of our being as humans. That is when forgiveness comes into play. People are not perfect! We have to accept that, but remember the commitment you made to each other and before God. Commitment means being dedicated and having loyalty no matter what happens. A man who professes to be after God's own heart should not break a commitment to the one God gave him! Can I say that again? A man who is after God's own heart should not break a commitment to the one God gave to him, meaning his wife!

Now, understanding that we both would mess up because we are flesh and no one is perfect, the commitment should still never waver. Try asking your partner, as I did, "Did God send you to me?" Listen very carefully to his answer, and know that a woman claiming to live in God's will for her life should have the same mentality. Never give up! God did His part so you do yours. It took a second marriage for me to receive that lesson. We must continuously ask ourselves, "Am I continuing to live in the will of God?" We must also know we will fall short, but it's what we do when that happens that matters. Get back up again or stay down?

So in the beginning, I did indeed think, *Twenty-six-year age difference? Not in this lifetime*, but God orchestrated a different plan and was working it out for my good. I also knew myself and that finding true love a second time was rare, or so I thought. I had only had two other serious relationships in my life. As I explained earlier, I was married once before for ten years (after dating for ten years) and was single for about eleven and a half years after that. But I knew that I was supposed to be married.

When my first marriage did not work out, I began to think about marriage differently and did some research. I also needed to understand my part in the ending of my marriage. I had to really seek God because I knew He was not pleased and that He hated divorce and it was a threat to the social order that He created. For in Malachi 2:16a, He says, "For I hate putting away, saith Jehovah, the God of Israel." I truly believe we were unequally yoked in many areas and that God forgave me for my part in it and led me in that decision to end it. So who am I to judge others on if they are believers or not? I can only go by how they choose to live their lives according to what a believer does, right? So my soul was at peace because I tried very hard to keep my marriage, but one cannot do it alone. I realize, looking back, I actually stayed longer than I should have. Oh, but God! He gave me confirmation through, of all things, my child. Not only was my safety and sanity at risk but hers was also. Once we left the situation, the actual noticeable difference in my daughter was like night and day, and it was the only confirmation I needed to keep going. So moving forward with God's help, we survived, and God actually called me to that peace that surpasses all understanding. Believe me, I did not understand it. And I thank Him for never giving up on me and for forgiving me! God never left us, and His love got us through.

Now over the years, I came to understand the different types of love that are required in a marriage. Getting into God's Word and also watching other couples whom I respected gave me lessons to live by. More important, I learned how to do it in God's eyes. What I found opened my eyes, and I realized the type of love I was giving in my first marriage

4

was hindering and not allowing our relationship to prosper. Again, trying to figure out my part in what happened, I had to understand how to love. And loving bad behavior is not the answer, especially if you go in thinking you will be loved as Christ loves you. That was one of my biggest mistakes.

In God's eyes, there is Eros love, the romantic and sexual love, which seeks sensual expression. Then there is Philia love, where companionship, communication, and cooperation play out through friendship. And last but not least, there is the agape love, the self-giving love where you make it happen no matter what the other person does, which is the hardest but can be attained in Christ. Breaking down all these different types or ways to love helped me understand what it means to love, and I now know that commitment is crucial when doing it God's way.

We also have to have an understanding of our differences and similarities because we end up marrying someone who is both opposite and similar to us. We had to adjust to both. My honey pastor and I were not only different in age but in many other ways. Think about this: we actually married for our similarities, and we stay together for our differences. That fact blew my mind, but really, we do. Once I understood that, my mindset changed. I realized that being different is rarely the cause of conflict in marriages; the problems arise from our similarities. It's ironic because most times the similarities draw us together. The differences pique our interest at first, and we want to know more about the other person because we have never experienced those things. The differences are the occasion; similarities are the cause. We must understand that we can't change a person into who we want him or her to be. So we should not try to eliminate the difference by demanding, pressuring, or manipulating the other person. I did that and found out that it will not work, for the Bible says in Ephesians

4:2, "with all lowliness and meekness, with longsuffering, forbearing one another in love." That is how we should handle our differences, always in love.

Learning to accept what we consider the good and the bad is part of commitment in any relationship. I had to turn to God in those moments to help me see what was best. He truly does know what is best for His children so I had to rebuke my way for the man He sent to get me. God helped me know that neither his age nor his vocation mattered because his heart was for God.

Consider This

Decisions in God's will are always challenging for us in our flesh. When He gives what we asked for, He is patiently waiting on our reaction to accepting it.

STAGE 2

The Reverend Was Chasing, and I Was Running, but God Was Working It Out

So God sent him, and did I dismiss him after meeting him the first time? Yes, I did—or I tried to. I must admit he made an impression. It was not a good one but a memorable one nevertheless. Why was I trying to ignore it? Because I did not like him. We met at a church ironically through one of my good friends. He seemed to be full of himself (my first impression), and I did not appreciate the way he treated my friend. I have to admit that he was very handsome and distinguished with gray in his mustache and some around his hairline. He was charismatic, and he smelled good, but I saw an elderly (although he did not look old), fresh gentleman whose actions toward my friend I did not care for. Notice I said, "smelled good." There is just something about a good-smelling man. At any rate, that day, I came to spend time with my friend, who was having a bad day, and I wished he would leave us alone. He was also a minister at that point, having left the position of a pastor years prior, and some pastors had the reputation of not living holy in their actions. Sad but true, and, yes, I put him in that particular category because of stereotypes. Was that wrong of me? Yes, it was, but I did it. Remembering we should not judge is hard when you have an opinion about something that you know is wrong and not of God and you have seen it with your own eyes. The perception that a man of God is a god and should be treated as such was real, which took respect to a whole other level.

So I fell into the wrong way of thinking. Again, I acknowledge it was wrong but real! For the Bible says, "A man's goings are established of Jehovah; And he delighteth in his way." Psalm 37:23. As it was, he had to show me his steps for me to come around to a different way or God's way of thinking about him.

His age and his vocation made me think that I should look the other way and not even go there. I also was not about casually dating at that point in my life. I had been divorced for eleven and a half years and was not into playing games in a relationship. I never was into that, to tell the truth. I was raising my daughter alone and had only had one semiserious—or so I thought—relationship during that time. It lasted about two years, off and on, and turned out to be about fun and games for the other party, which would not work. Thank you, God, for showing me that when I finally got ready to listen! That was another example of God not leaving or forsaking me in my own mess. I realized that I created it, and He did not. Amen! So if and when God sent someone for real, and I knew He would because I was supposed to be married, as I was domestic by nature, I had to be ready for the real and forget the mess. And whomever God sent had to be ready to settle down with me and accept my daughter.

After all my assumptions, later, I was reminded of the Lord saying to Samuel, "For man looketh on the outward appearance, but the Jehovah looketh on the heart" 1 Samuel 16:7c. Even though I was not trying to look at his heart, let alone spend time with him, he kept coming. I realize that God was telling him to!

While I was visiting my friend at her office one day, he kept finding reasons to come and talk to her the whole time I was there. I tried hard to ignore his presence, but I have to admit, it was strong in that it was like he was being presented to me for some reason. Little did I know that God was working it out for my good. Was I called to visit my friend for this purpose? "And we know that to them that love God all things work together for good, even to them that are called according to his purpose" Romans 8:28.

A couple of days later, my friend told me he asked about me. About a week later, she told me again. Some time went by, and she told me he wanted to meet me. To my surprise, he never forgot me. Even then, I asked her why, because I couldn't do anything with that old man, and I didn't like him or his attitude on that day we met. She said, "Just talk to him because he seemed serious."

Now I knew that I had taken time and made my wishes known to God. I was practicing ACTS at that time, and I still do in my prayer life. I was *acknowledging* God for who He was in my life, *confessing* my sins to Him and asking for forgiveness, giving *thanks* for everything He was and allowed in my life, and giving my *supplications* to Him for His guidance. So He knew what I wanted at the same time knowing what I needed because the Word says, "And there is no creature that is not manifest in his sight: but all things are naked and laid open before the eyes of him with whom we have to do" Hebrews 4:13. I had surrendered, and God saw me, right? So was God in His majesty telling me it was time? Was I really ready to get into another relationship? That was what I had to figure out. So I submitted and allowed the Holy Spirit to lead. It is a hard thing to get out of your own way, but you must.

After a few months went by, he still never forgot me. I relented and told my friend to give him my number. She did, and he called. The first night he called, we talked until the next morning. It was like we had known each other for years, and I was pleasantly shocked—not surprised but shocked! Why? I don't know because I had talked to God, right? See, that is it: our flesh is always there to try to take us off course. That is when we must take heed of the Holy Spirit and rebuke the flesh even if it does not look like we think it should look. Oh but God!

I have always been drawn to older people. Maybe it was because my mother had me when she was older. I'm not sure. But older men I knew who had experience seemed to have gotten all the foolishness out of their systems because they had lived. He was nothing like I thought. Again, it had to be God who stepped in because after that night, I begin to think maybe this one was someone I needed to get to know more about. He was not one to just walk away from. The conversation was just that powerful and full of something. I mean, we talked all night long and into the next morning with no lull in the conversation. It just flowed! I believe God was saying, "What did you ask Me for? No one told you not to be specific in your asking." And I did not mention age, a vocation, or one who was not arrogant. It was like God was saying, "Did you?" He turned out not to be arrogant at all; he was just confident in himself and who he had become in Christ. Imagine that? I asked for a man of God who would accept me and my mess and who would become the head of my household and be a father figure to my child. So God said, "You go back and look deeper." And I hung my head as if to be chastised and became obedient to my Father.

Consider This

Be careful what you ask God for, and remember, first impressions are almost never what they seem. Be cautious, but dig deeper.

STAGE 3

They Said, "Don't Do It" (Was It Christian Love or Messy Church Folks?)

After some time of getting to know him, I chose to tell someone about how serious we were about each other. Why I did that, I don't know. I guess I was thinking that as I was active in the church and spending time in ministry and fellowship that my character was known so I would get some Godly advice. But that did not happen. When I told people that I was going to marry him, almost everyone said, "Don't you marry that old man!" I had to remember that I thought that very same thing in the beginning, only looking on the outside. I also knew that not everybody would be happy for me. So I kind of expected some responses because it had not been that long. I was kind of prepared for the negativity from some but not from the church, especially those who had gotten to know him. I later realized that my first mistake was telling anyone. They all seemed to only be looking at that outer appearance. No one wanted to look any deeper at the man or what I felt I needed in my life. Even my dear mother, may she rest in peace, was not happy about my decision, which I expected. I knew how she felt about men, period, and now her baby was involved with one who was close to her age. No, ma'am, she was not having any part of that! But I had to remember that when people depart, no matter who they are, "God is our refuge and strength, a very present help in trouble" Psalm 46:1, even if the trouble was not for me because I could look past the opinions at this point. I was a grown woman living on my own and raising my child in my own home.

There was really no issue for us because God had ordained this relationship in the first place. The problem would occur if we allowed those outside of our relationship to be involved. That can cause trouble, which is something that you must recognize and deal with when you are in a relationship. It was only God's divine interference that allowed me to go forth, explore the possibility of it, and eventually say yes. So really I was being obedient to what I asked God to do in my life for me and my child. Lesson learned! Keep folks out of your relationship. Only invite God. But God, true to who He is, worked it all out. He allowed members of my church to see who my future husband really was, and they began to love him and invited him to teach Sunday school, which they so enjoyed. Some thought he would join our church. As God would have it, that was not the plan.

Now, back to keeping God in our relationship. I had to keep in mind the Word says, "Therefore shall a man leave his father and his mother, and shall cleave unto his wife: and they shall be one flesh" Genesis 2:24. Did you catch that? We tend to not see the emphasis in that scripture or we look over it. The man leaves Daddy and Momma and cleaves to his wife, not the public, whether the church or not. Although *cleave* has two opposite meanings, in this scripture, it means "to join oneself to." So the man is given another mandate to follow from God. Now I understand that some people believe that when you marry, you also marry the family. That is not true. Acceptance is on everybody, but first and foremost, it begins with the man and woman. They have to fight for each other and create a strong bond in their relationship, with God included, so no person can separate them. It starts at home, and eventually, if God is in it, everyone else will come around. But if they don't, that is okay also. I thank God that most did!

We knew there might be some family who would have reservations about the person their family member chose to marry, whether warranted or not. They might think they were just looking out for their loved one. To keep confusion down, one could go into it being open and honest about any reservations and just have a conversation, which was the approach I took. I knew that allowing God to intervene in that and with much prayer, all would be well in that area. I did not meet any of his family until after we got married, for whatever reason or, I like to think, as God would have it. Remember, God knows all and will work it out if you get out of the way and allow it to happen in His time.

Going forward, three things happened, which I won't mention because they were for me and what God has for you is for you. But after the third thing happened, I surrendered and said, "Okay, God, I hear You, and with You, I can do this. So let's go to work and make it happen." From that point on, I knew I had to keep folk out of my head, and I never looked back. I always knew the Holy Spirit was with us, for His Word stated, "And I will pray the Father, and he shall give you another Comforter, that he may abide in you for ever" John 14:16. Forever! Yes, we must remember, if God brings you to something, He is still there in it with you, for He also said, "I will in no wise fail thee, neither will I in any wise forsake thee" Hebrews 13:5b.

There were also lessons I learned from previous relationships. One is that marriage should only be between those two involved with God's guidance and should not include family, friends, or acquaintances, *ever*—not even children or the pastor except for counseling purposes, but not the church. That should be a rule of thumb and should never change until death do you part. Marriage is hard enough. Ask anyone who is married, and he or she will tell you that. Throw in a significant age difference and a man of the cloth, and hard can become impossible, if you allow it. So having others enter into it with you is a big, big no-no. I can't say it enough.

Communication between two partners is not only key; it should never stop. It really is crucial in any relationship. Communication in marriage is like what blood is to life. It is impossible to have any kind of relationship unless there is constant communication. This is true for you and your fiancé and for your individual relationship with God. You not only need to talk to each other but you must listen to each other as well. Paying attention and listening to what the other person says means accepting it and how he or she feels but not judging him or her for feeling that way or for even saying it. You don't have to agree, but acknowledge what the other person is going through. Remember, for that person, it is real. And both must understand that your words publicize the state of your heart. In Luke 6:45, we are told, "The good man out of the good treasure of his heart bringeth forth that which is good; and the evil man out of the evil treasure bringeth forth that which is evil: for out of the abundance of the heart his mouth speaketh." Once something is said, it can't be taken back. So we should choose our words wisely. It can be hard, but both of you must make the effort. Try not to let your tongue cut the other person.

The Word of God gives the best instructions on communication. In Proverbs 18:13, it says, "He that giveth answer before he heareth, It is folly and shame unto him." And James 1:19 tells us, "Ye know this, my beloved brethren. But let every man be swift to hear, slow to speak, slow to wrath." Now, see Proverbs 21:2–3: "Every way of a man is right in his own eyes; But Jehovah weigheth the hearts. To do righteousness and justice is more acceptable to Jehovah than sacrifice." The head and the heart are not always on the same page, so getting them lined up is our daily challenge. Doing what is right is God's way and not our way or our spouse's way. Remember, God weighs the heart and sees the action that follows. What a great example to follow and live by, right?

I learned that I did not want to disappoint God more than I did not want to disappoint my husband. Being disappointed is a state of mind for humans, and we can get over it. However, to disappoint God is a different kind of ball game. That kind will hit you in your soul, and until that is right, you won't be.

Once communication breaks down or stops, the oneness is over. That is when Satan is allowed in to do his bidding, which is to kill, steal, and destroy. We, unknowingly or maybe knowingly, sometimes invite him in to cause more damage to the mess that we started. For we act as if we are what the Word says in John 8:44a: "Ye are of your father the devil, and the lusts of your father it is your will to do." We are human and have those moments, but we have to tune out any evil and other forces—be it Momma, other family, and especially church folks—in order to hear God's voice. Remember, it's your relationship. Make it yours, you two only. We did, and our wedding date was set.

Consider This

Invite God and *no* one else into your marriage, and allow Him to take a seat and stay, not to observe but to guide and contribute. Then you both follow His lead.

STAGE 4

Preparing for "I Do" (Focusing on God, Not Outside Negative Interference)

It was eight months to the first day we met. Was it quick? Yes, it was to some who only thought about our age difference. They made that the main focus. *Focus* is the operative word here. We were only concerned about us and if we were equally yoked as believers. That was *our* focus. God's Word says, "Be not unequally yoked with unbelievers: for what fellowship have righteousness and iniquity? or what communion hath light with darkness?" 2 Corinthians 6:14. Since we both had done this before, having the same belief system and serving the same God was much more important to us than any age difference. I believe that we both realized at some point in our prior marriages we did not focus on that fact as much as we should have. That was a big mistake on my part. I slipped into what Amy wanted instead of staying in what God wanted for me within His will. I told myself, "This time, stay in your belief system!" I had come to learn that in sustaining a relationship, let alone a marriage, there were differences that could have been red flags. And in those differences, sometimes, I chose to try to change them for my good not God's. "Amy, this time, stay in your belief system!"

Moving forward, I had to make sure I truly did marriage God's way because I wanted this to be the last time I said, "I do." To do that, I thought it would help to start at the beginning—you know, take a retrospective look. I looked back to when we first met, when I was an active, worshipping member of the African Methodist Episcopal (AME) Church. My daughter and I were deeply involved in ministry on a regular basis throughout the year, traveling here and there in support of the church in our ministries. He was an active, worshipping member of the Baptist Church. Now I grew up in the Baptist Church, and we both served the same true and living God. "For to this end we labor and strive, because we have our hope set on the living God, who is the Saviour of all men, specially of them that believe" 1 Timothy 4:10. That verse was how you could describe each of us in our walk with Christ. We both were true believers, though we knew that there was a difference in the structure of our churches. That happened to be okay with us because we served the same God and believed in His Son, Jesus the Christ, and His resurrection. That foundation was in place. God was working it out.

The proof of that for me was when we decided to go through premarital counseling as a way of helping us both, even though we both had been married before. It was needed because even if you think you have the spiritual side in check in your relationship, the fleshly side is alive and well and needs help too. And understand that the spiritual side will be attacked. I was so grateful and a little surprised that he agreed to go and explore that with me, which gave me another reason to love him. We understood that premarital counseling was important no matter what age either of us was. Because two people coming together from different families have different expectations concerning marriage based on their individual upbringings and, in our case, other marriages and our ages. It helps couples deal with conflict or the damaged emotions that may follow chronic disappointment in each other. We know that some type of disappointment will come and go. Because premarital counseling has godly intent, it prepared us because this time we were seeking to enter into a marriage relationship based on sacrificial love for one another and to place the needs of the other before our own. Most important, it taught us the truth about marriage according to the Word of God. Christian couples are encouraged to invite Jesus Christ to be not only a personal Savior but also the third cord in their union spoken of in Ecclesiastes 4. We should always include Jesus by making Him an integral partner or the main focus in our marriage. Those were concepts we had discussed in our counseling sessions. Some we knew, and some were eye-openers, even for us. Yes, even the pastor, who had counseled many on marriage, learned a thing or two. What was important was that he was willing and there was something for him to learn because he as a man had failed at it before.

At this point, we both thought the other was sweet and cute and could do no wrong. Not! We knew that we might love each other, but there would be times when we would not like each other. Your partner is not you. He or she is created in God's image, not yours. And even though we are made in God's image, we take that image and mess it up with our own stuff! And we knew that we would not always look at each other through God's eyes. Each of us has a right to be who we are in Christ or not. Each should be treated with respect. We needed to respect each other's differences by actively making conscience efforts to do so—those that *can't be* changed, such as age, race, looks, and home and cultural background, and those that *can be* changed, like personal habits, your mindset, and the way you do things.

I had to be mindful that making any changes in myself would be my idea but led by God, not by my husband. To change for someone else's sake and not for your own good can lead to more trouble in your marriage. Allow God to instruct you on any area that needs work in you. I had to, and still do, believe and admit that I need work. That is a constant. Do not believe for a second that you can change a person or that another person can change you. It will not work. I know because I tried it. Listen, in relationships, there will be some doubt. It comes from being in our own feelings, which come and go. They change often. I had to remember that. Yes, a touch or kiss causes us to quiver, which is not a bad thing, but feelings or emotions can cause us to mess up, thinking we are so in love and all is peaches and cream. That can be when we lose focus.

I found that losing focus on God putting you together and serving Him before you serve each other can cause some major problems in marriages—that is, if God brought you to it in the first place. If He did, He has to remain the main focus, period. We need to give God the credit He deserves when he answers our prayers. *Human fellowship is great but must not come before or replace spiritual fellowship.* Make an effort to remember to never lose focus on God as the Head, which keeps Him as part of your union.

And so, on June 21, 2003, with no big fanfare, in my pastor's office with only witnesses, a total of five including my daughter by my side, we said, "I do." For better or worse, Father God, help us to follow Your lead in this one.

Consider This

Believing that God put your marriage together should *never* change. Stay focused on that, and accept that you will be tested. Surviving the struggles is part of your commitment.

STAGE 5

Did He Really Take Me as His Wife? (Showpiece as the First Lady or Helpmeet?)

Now, with him being twenty-six years older than I was, I had to ask myself, "Does he truly desire a real wife as a helpmeet, or does he just want a pretty young thang to have as a showpiece?" Remember, I was domestic, and my nature was to take care of people, so cooking, cleaning, and nurturing as a wife was in me, and I enjoyed it. For me, being a helpmeet at home was good and somewhat different from being a helpmeet in the church. So I was thinking he had to include me in ministry as he served God's people. Would he do that? That was my concern. I thought about growing up seeing and hearing about how pastors in general would always put the church and its members before their families. That was actually real. The perception about preacher's kids (PKs) being bad or staying in trouble because of getting no attention from the father who was the pastor was where it came from. It seemed he would never have time for the children or family as such. Later, I will dig deeper into the wife making sure there is time for the family.

I knew I was meant to be a helpmeet as a wife but what about a helpmeet as the first lady? Was there a difference? I did not know. It was foreign to me. Did he even consider that or think about how it should look? I had to ask the question. In my mind, I came up with all kinds of situations that could be placed before us. He had been married before for many years, so this time, following God in choosing someone younger meant what for him and the church? I had to make sure that God had ordained it for us to be together, not only from my perspective but from his as well. What was I really walking into as far as him being the pastor? Did I truly understand it? As it turned out, it was totally different from what I thought, and I did not fully understand nor was I prepared for this new venture.

When we met, he was no longer a full-time pastor. However, he was on staff and very active in the church with Sunday school as the minister of Christian education. As I stated before, he was charismatic and carried himself in a way that you knew he was a pastor or a man of God. When we would go out, people would stop and ask him all the time if he was a pastor because I believe the anointing showed on and through him. God also showed me that he would pastor again because that was what he was. It was in him, and that was his purpose. He reminded me of the old-time preachers who really cared about the people, who were there for the people in their actions, not just when it was expected because of the title of pastor. He was passionate about teaching the Word of God to all people inside the classroom and in how he carried himself. He actually lived what he taught. He was the example. He would always say that your sermon should be your life; it should be lived. So the question was how would I fit into that equation of being his wife and the first lady? Only God could answer that for me. So lesson learned, always turn to God for guidance. We have a lot of opinions, but God has the actual answer. I just had to take heed and be obedient to His solution.

Before we got married, we made the decision to remain members of our separate churches. Wow, did we hear much from others about how we should be at the same church as husband and wife or especially that I, as the wife, should be with my husband. In the beginning, we saw no need to change because we served the same God and were active in our respective churches. Speaking of respective churches, we knew we had to decide which one we would join to become members in the same congregation. In the end, we chose to listen to God for any decision about moving our memberships and when to do it. We thought it best considering we had a young child involved, and we did not want to just uproot from her church just because we said, "I do." Her spiritual walk was important to us also. We had no doubt that the God we served would work that out for us as a family.

During that time, God did not tell either of us to move, so we didn't. We would visit each other from time to time. He even taught Sunday school at my church a few times and was considering moving to the AME church with me. Oh, but God had a different plan. We had been married for about four years when God brought it to pass. He began to accept invitations to visit churches that needed a pastor. As his wife, I was right by his side. Going on these visits gave me an idea of what being a pastor's wife could be like in the mission field. It gave me hope that we would and could work well together in ministry. God allowed me to see how we could make a difference in those churches and their communities. My head was turning with ideas for actively starting mission projects in the future. That was when I began to ask questions because I knew our life as it was would change forever. And boy, did it change but not in the way I thought!

Over the years, I came to know that wives, or I should say women in general, understand love as our driving need, meaning we need to feel it to know it's real. And when that need is met, we are happy, but without love, we react without respect. Some of us—and it took me a minute to get it—don't really understand that, but it is real. Ephesians 5:22 says, "Wives, be in subjection unto your own husbands, as unto the Lord." "As unto the Lord" is the important part of that scripture. Wives, we must ask ourselves, especially when our husband is not acting God-like, whether he is the pastor or not, do I respect, love, and submit unto the Lord first and follow suit treating my husband the same way? Not as a god but as "the head"? I did not do that in my first marriage. My mistake was stepping into head mode, thinking I could fix the situation and my ex-spouse.

Now when your spouse is not treating you as God treats the church that is the hardest lesson to learn and live by. In my mind, I believe that respect is reciprocal; if you want it, you must give it. So if someone lashes out in anger, frustration, or whatever, he or she should be prepared to receive the same in return, right? We know that even the most loving and gentle man or woman can take only so much of another's bad attitude when in the flesh. In any relationship one will be treated badly at some point. We all have bad days, but remember, they won't and shouldn't last. Did I learn that lesson? Yes, in time, I did, and it was still hard but doable, though only with God's help.

Looking at husbands or men in general, I learned that they understand respect. That is their one driving need, to feel respected. However, again, I didn't always do that, and I still stumble in that area at times. The flesh is real. But understand that when that need is met, he is happy and can function in a Christ-like manner. Without respect, especially from his wife, he will react without love and do some of the dumbest stuff. He will forget to "Let thy fountain be blessed; And rejoice in the wife of thy youth" Proverbs 5:18. We must always remember the following: "one that ruleth well his own house, having *his* children in subjection with all gravity; (but if a man knoweth not how to rule his own house, how shall he take care of the church of God?)" 1 Timothy 3:4–5. That is God's way. When the husband and wife operate outside what the Word of God has designed for them, things get crazy. Unfortunately, a lot of marriages stay in that crazy phrase for way too long. My first marriage did, and it was because I did not really understand my role as a wife, so I was in that crazy mode too long. I thought at that point the lesson was learned, but it really wasn't. It did not click just yet. I was still trying to run things for me and him. Surrendering to God for help was what I needed then and always. It took some time after that realization, but I learned the lesson, so this time would be better. It would not be perfect but better because that was one important lesson.

We should never strive for perfection. It does not exist because we are fleshly creatures. We have to mess up in order to learn. I knew that! In a sense, that would be setting yourself up for failure. Only God is perfect.

So if he understands respect as a man and I understand love as a woman, would we be a good fit as pastor and wife for the church or just husband and wife? Only God could answer either of those questions. The other main characteristic was he as the man must love me as Christ loves the church and his people. Then the submission on my, the woman's part, should fall into place. I always understood that marriage was full of challenges and that it would be work. It was up to me or us to make it a good work to please God. Having love and commitment as your foundation can help in making the work good.

Then in all this, I questioned how he as the pastor would present us as a team, which would set the tone and make all the difference in our ministry. What I found was it did not happen that way. I had to take my expectations out and allow God in His time to show me what would happen when I was not allowed to walk by his side. That was when I had to turn to God and say, "Take the wheel. I now surrender him, this situation, and myself in it to You."

Consider This

Love should be something one does and not something one only says occasionally. It's an action shown over and over again as a lifestyle.

STAGE 6

Becoming the Right Person for My Husband (It Was Never about Me!)

There's a saying that goes something like this: "Don't try to marry the right person; instead, try becoming the right person for someone else." Being honest about who you are by God's standard is the first step to becoming the right person. "If we say that we have no sin, we deceive ourselves, and the truth is not in us," but know that God promised in His Word that "if we confess our sins, he is faithful and righteous to forgive us our sins, and to cleanse us from all unrighteousness" 1 John 1:8, 9. And I know that God does not lie. So why not choose to acknowledge and confess the sin and make a conscious choice to work on it, especially if it can be forgiven and one can be cleansed at the same time? Remember, we are children of God first and should want to please our Father in what we do. How could I be worthy in that same right as his wife and helpmeet in God's eyes? I really wanted to please my husband as God would have it. To become what my husband needed was my goal. So with that in mind, I had to work on myself and my mess that I already had from previous relationships.

I had to get rid of some stuff while deciding what to keep for God to use in my marriage through me. It would require work on my part because being single for so long, one would develop some bad habits, and of course, I did. Living the way I did would have to change, and I welcomed that change because it would be for the best.

I always knew marriage was not about me. Marriage is about the other person. I truly believe that. A lot of marriages don't last because people don't believe that is true. The days of thinking in terms of me and mine were over. Me and mine would become us and ours. When I said, "I do," the sooner I begin to think and live in those terms, the better off both of us would be. Think of it like this: when decisions need to be made, you can no longer make them alone, because once you marry, those same decisions now involve your spouse as well. Every decision made would affect our household. One might say, "But I am an individual." Yes, you are, so is he, but each of you being a whole person with your own goals and ministry will make for a better contribution to a solid relationship with Christ as the center. I knew I had to bring something to the table. That something had to be of substance, and it would be as if I was taking it to God first.

I had been married, and my goal the second time, if God blessed me to do it again, was for this to be the last time because this time, it would be different. I would allow God to lead and send my husband to get me and not go get what I wanted. That was another task, preparing myself in my new singleness all over again. Would it be easy? No, because it was new and anything new is always a challenge. We know whenever you become determined to do God's will, Satan is waiting to destroy you and all your plans. Also, I believe the first time I was married, I became an enabler, so I knew not to do that again. I learned that thinking you are helping someone to grow by not making him or her accountable for his or her bad behavior is not beneficial to any relationship, let alone a marriage. That was me being an enabler to my spouse. I truly learned that both parties have to be responsible for their own actions and growth first in order to bring something to a relationship or to be able to hold the other accountable—a whole person so to speak—but with God, all mistakes could be worked through for growth in Christ. We must remember "for it is God who worketh in you both to will and to work, for his good pleasure" Philippians 2:13. Sometimes we fight what God is trying to do in us, and I did that.

I had to admit though after being single for so long and head of the household, it was challenging for me to relinquish the power over my household, going from "my" to "our." I truly had to fight daily to submit to him as the head of the house.

I believe he also had a hard time understanding how the transition to him being the head of the household would play out. He did not want to step on my toes and especially not the toes of my daughter. He once stated that he understood that he was coming into her territory. So we made the decision to sit down and literally have a conversation as a family about the transition that was about to take place. Looking back, we really had to because he was moving into the house my daughter and I shared alone for about five years. We set up ground rules and went through different scenarios to see what each of us thought and how we felt we could deal with them should they arise. Again, communication was and is key in any relationship, whether it be with a new husband or an existing child. Just know that all parties have to be included. No one should feel uncomfortable in his or her own home. And now this would be a house we all called home.

Another thing is that expectations should be based on what you say and how you carry out what you say—meaning show what you mean, and if you change your mind, say that too. Everyone is entitled to change—it's a part of growing—but in a relationship, it should be shared with the other person. The two who become one should grow together, not apart, and that includes any changes either feels the need to make. And if you choose not to grow with your partner, speak those things as if they were so. Do not act on those things as if they were so to the surprise of your partner and everyone else. We forget that relationships require work, from beginning to end. That old saying "The same thang it took to get your baby, it's gonna take to keep her or him" is true. Don't say you want one if you don't, and if you change your mind about the relationship, say so to your partner. It will save a lot of heartache on both parts, which sometimes hurts other family members who suffer also, like children. They watch everything you do, and they have their own feelings about it. The words "till death do us part" mean until one of you dies.

Please understand that including God in your ceremony and saying the words is good and all, but choosing to go against those words is damnation to God and disrespect against your partner. Try not to forget that you are attempting to become the "right" person in Christ.

Yes, there will be disagreements. You will not like each other all the time, but love and respect should remain at all times. I had to learn that putting on an appearance for the sake of others and keeping down confusion would happen. Did I like it? No! I have never been good at being fake or pretending to be someone I am not, but I have come to learn that compromise keeps the peace in many a situation. I still have to work on this one. Remember, being right is not the goal. So when contributing to your home and your marriage, never stop looking to God for answers on how you are doing. The work should never stop; that is part of the adventure of honoring what God put together. Looking inward at ourselves, which is where God looks, can and will make all the difference in how we become the right person for our spouse.

Consider This

You can only give to another if you are whole in Christ. Always make a continuous effort to work on yourself even when you become one.

STAGE 7

Add a Twelve-Year-Old to the Equation (Inclusion in Blending Required Much Attention and Time)

Three months after we met, I had a conversation with my daughter, who was approaching thirteen years old and going into her teenage years. It was time for her to be let in on what was going on with her mother because my relationship was just that serious. Her hormones were raging about becoming a teenager, which is a new challenge in itself. Now her mother had met someone, really, and he was old enough to be her grandfather? In fact, he was a friend of her paternal grandfather's. And it had been just she and I for the last eleven and a half years of me being a single parent. As a rule, I never introduced anyone I went out with to her unless I thought he would be around for a while, so after three months, was I really thinking about introducing someone and talking marriage? That was how hard this whole relationship hit me. I truly understood that a child's character could be built or influenced by what he or she saw his or her parents do or not do.

She had only met one other person before, and it did not work out. Alternatively, I really did not give her any voice in that relationship. Maybe that was a sign from God, to not include her in that one because He knew it was not for us. I knew if she had reservations, which was a very real possibility, we would have to rethink this thing. I knew at that point she was the only entity who would've stopped anything from going any further. So her reaction was important to me. However, I also realized that in our case, God would work that out as well. The foundation for righteousness had been laid. So when it got serious, I had to get in her head to see how she felt about the situation because we were a package deal. She needed to understand that there was no way I could leave her out of my decision and that God would not even allow that. I mean, this man was coming into our home, and that was her safe place. We talked about me not being with her father, which did not mean I would be alone for the rest of my life. I also tried to make her understand that she was and always would be very important in my decisions concerning myself because she was a part of me, and only God came before her. Her reaction was just as I thought it would be. She already had a quiet, nonchalant, keep-to-myself type of personality, and that was exactly what I got. But she seemed to listen, and I truly believe she knew I would not let any hurt or harm come to her and she would be safe, so we set up a time for her to meet my future husband.

The time came for them to meet. He came over to our home one evening. He waited in the den as she came in from her bedroom. They exchanged pleasantries when she walked in, and he even shook her hand. She did not say much at first, which I expected. We had spoken about how even if she did not agree or like the situation, she had to always be respectful, and she was. Let's face it; we all knew there had to be an adjustment period. However, he came in the most respectful way possible. He came as a real man who understood her part in this whole equation. She would not be left out, and her opinion of him mattered to him. He dressed in a suit as if he were going to church and was so nervous, even sweating. I was not nervous because I truly believed that God had ordained this to happen. His actions made a big difference to me and proved again what type of man he was. We both knew this decision would not only change our lives but also that of an innocent preteen female child. Her relationship with her father was not ideal, but she had seen what a Christian married couple should look like in her grandparents, aunts, and uncles and couples at church. Was their meeting a hug-fest in the end? No. But God made me see it was to be. Confirmation once again!

We then had to discuss what my last name would be. This was important to me because I had been married before and I still had my ex-husband's last name. I wanted to keep his name for my daughter's sake. Having grown up with a different last name from my mother with no father in the house, I went through some situations with mean kids and wanted to prevent my child from experiencing that. When my fiancé and I talked about it, I found out he felt a certain kind of way as well because he grew up with a different last name from his mother and the father who raised him, his stepfather. Even though his stepfather was very loving toward him and did not treat him differently from his stepbrothers, he still had issues with his name being different from his other siblings in the same household. So we came up with a solution together. I would keep my name and hyphenate it to add his. Also confirmation was given years later, as my daughter felt some kind a way about it too. It made her feel included, as I found out from a conversation we had after someone called me Mrs. Coleman and not Mrs. Lee-Coleman in her presence. So from then on, especially when she was around, I would correct people. I was actually okay either way because I knew who I was, but because my daughter was still a child, I wanted her to be okay as well.

Now since she was very active at the church we attended, we had to discuss her coming with us and leaving her church home. Remember, she was a preteen dealing with her own hormones and peer pressure, so did we really want to take her away from her place of worship? With much prayer, we made another decision together that we thought would work for our situation.

God is so good, and He continues to give confirmation! He was working it out all along. A few years into our marriage, she began calling my honey pastor Daddy James just out of the blue. God did it through my husband, who came in and treated us as a family. It was so endearing that I began to praise God and my husband began to cry the first time my daughter called him that. Confirmation, confirmation, glory to God! I explained it was because of how he treated her, which was just like his own daughter. Again, actions speak so much louder than words. I got out of their way because God had already shown me that he would be a good father figure to her. So I just had to be patient and wait on God. As my favorite scripture says, "*Wait* for Jehovah: Be strong, and let thy heart take courage; Yea, *wait* thou for Jehovah" Psalm 27:14. My honey pastor came through that test with flying colors. He participated in school projects, picked her up when needed, and got her to where she needed to be when I could not do it.

I will never forget a project she worked on for school. It was about the family unit. There were questions for each family member, and when it came to the father, she went to him immediately for those responses. That really showed me how she actually felt about him living in the household. He was truly the father presence. When her friends came around, he was not just there but present. At her graduation, he was present. On the trip to drop her off at college, he was there and present. He planned and took us on family vacations as well.

He gave encouragement and answered her hopes and fears. He was the strong support she needed, showing patience, honesty, and loving-kindness.

As a family, we served the same God in our home and prayed together. The only thing that was missing was us attending the same church building as a family, and we had discussed that and how it would be before coming together, so that was okay too. But know that when my daughter was in a program at church, her stepfather was there, make no mistake about it. God in His time made it all work out. In His majesty, once again, He proved that keeping Him in your situation will allow things to work out for your good. So grateful was I!

Consider This

If God shows you how something should be for your life, *trust* that He will get all the important parties on board in His time and *not* yours. Wait on Him.

STAGE 8

What Does the Term First Lady Mean for Me and to Us?

As I stated before, I knew God would call my husband to pastor again, so I had to prepare myself for what that would look like as his wife. At some point, a new term would be bestowed upon me: *first lady.* That term came with a lot of expectations that I probably would not live up to. Who was I kidding? I knew I would not live up to them simply because of opinions already formed about me based on our age difference and coming from a different denomination. I had met many pastors' wives, and all of them were very different in their own way. I never expected or wanted them to be anyone other than who they were when I got to know them. However, there was an unwritten rule of how many Baptist churches wanted their first lady to be presented. I knew above all else I would be representing my husband in his role as pastor.

I remember my good friend's mother, who was a well-known and respected first lady, told me these three words: "You be Amy!" I took that to heart because that was all I knew how to be—the person God made me to be. And I would allow God to handle the rest, knowing it would not be easy for me in my own flesh.

I decided to do some research. So first, I looked up the term *first lady*. I knew what it meant in the black church, but I wanted to know where it came from. I also knew it was not biblical. There is no scripture that specifically explains what the pastor's wife or first lady should do or how she should act, per se. Therefore, that left me to believe that the pastor should define her role to her and for the church because she is his wife. But what do you do if that does not happen and you are thrown into what can seem like a lions' den? That is the reason you have to pray and ask God to help you define your role as His servant—not a title automatically given to you. Focus on that for yourself and no one else's expectations.

Now there are many scriptures that give instruction on how all Christian women should act and what they should and should not say, but for some reason, many do not believe that includes the first lady. Some churches have put the first lady in a peculiar place. They know how they want her to look and act at all times. They actually have created dos and don'ts based on their wants and expectations. She dare not have a relationship with God and submit to His will for her life if it does not meet their standards. I later found this to be the hardest lesson to come to terms with. Why is that? I do not know, but again, I wanted to know how the term came to be. So I asked some of the clergy and Sunday school teachers I respected and I even asked my husband. Boy, did I get a bunch of different scriptures and advice, and none of it was identical, made sense, or clicked in my mind! However, my honey pastor told me that it was not scriptural, which I knew, and that it came from churches creating what they thought the pastor's wife should be whether she was or not, but they mostly based it on Proverbs 31:10–31. So I asked, "Shouldn't those scriptures apply to all women who are married?" His answer was yes. So why is the pastor's wife different? Because in those scriptures, the Proverbs 31 woman is very busy doing the will of God and not being a showpiece? And term *first lady* is not mentioned. No one is first. What is mentioned is that her children and husband call her "blessed." So why not call her the "blessed lady" or "blessed wife" of the pastor or church? And note, it ends in verse 31 by saying, "Give her of the fruit of her hands; and let her own works praise her in the gates." That verse and the preceding verses tell me that she should use her hands to work in God's kingdom. Work requires action, right? These are specific instructions for all women who love the Lord and want to live for Him in their marriages so that they will be blessed.

And so my research continued. Again, biblically, I could not find anything specific. However, I did find the following based on one conversation with a pastor and his wife. They mention the term "elect lady" found in 2 John 1:1. After reading it, I understood it to be referring to the church and her members when it says, "unto the elect lady and her children." Even with that scripture, if it were referring to the pastor's wife, why not call her the "elect lady" or "chosen lady" of the pastor or church? Some churches do refer to the pastor's wife as the elect lady. Maybe that could be considered some biblical proof of the term for them.

Moving back to Genesis 2:18, where it states, "And Jehovah God said, It is not good that the man should be alone; I will make him a help meet for him." Again, that is for all women or helpmeets for men, right?

While birthing the Ministers' Wives Ministry at the church, as the coordinator, I drew on what I had learned while serving at the AME church, which was that there were different Hebrew words that translated to mean "help." For instance, the Hebrew term *ezer* is actually based on an ancient word *azar*. The *Strong's Hebrew Dictionary* translates it as "to surround, i.e. protect or aid:—help, succour." Now the word *succor* means to be the one who gives assistance in a time of great difficulty. See, God knew the husband, whether pastor or not, would have difficult times and he would need assistance, which explains the need for a helpmeet. We must understand that God called the wife to be so much more than just a helper to her husband. The world needs the gifts that God has stored on the inside of the wife.

When God gave the commission to subdue the earth, Eve was not excluded from the mandate. Genesis 1:28a says, "And God blessed them: and God said unto them, Be fruitful, and multiply, and replenish the earth, and subdue it." See the word *them*? It does not say *he* or *she* but *them*.

That is the Word of God. We understand that God wants the man and woman to come together and work as one. That may be the only time that the age thing would play a vital part in how one is accepted or treated. It would be up to that person and his or her upbringing, so to speak, having lived life in such a way that it would be hard to compromise. But with God, all things are possible. I have found that the pastor wants to please the people as much as he can within the realm of God's Word and not so much his wife. Her being secondary to God is one thing, but moving down the totem pole below the church and the members is a real challenge. However, it is a part of the life. Let's get back to the term *first lady*.

With Google being so popular in this day and age, I decided to do a Google search, and the only other place I found this term was in the political realm. However, I did not find any governmental documentation that said it was an official title. I learned that Martha Washington was called "first lady" by someone other than her husband, our first president, George Washington (1732–1799). In fact, it happened in a news article forty years after her death. Also there are those who stated that during the 1849 state funeral of Dolley Madison, the wife of James **Madison** (1809-1817), the fourth president of the United States, President Zachary Taylor (1849-1850), who wrote her eulogy called her "First Lady" while reciting it. And the first documented use of the term *first lady* in reference to the woman in charge of the White House was actually applied to a woman who was never married to a president. She was Harriet Lane, niece of President James Buchanan (1857–1861) and the official hostess for the only bachelor president. Lucy Hayes, wife of President Rutherford B. Hayes (1877–1881), was the first presidential wife to be introduced in a public speech as "first lady," by her husband.

Those were the first recorded times in the United States that the term was used. So that leads me to assume that the church took it from those examples and made it what they wanted it to be. In researching other areas, I found that the main role of any wife is to support her husband. She should watch out for him and try to be the place where he can relax from any stresses, whether from the church or elsewhere. However, he must allow her to do so. If not, she can only be available when needed and not take it personally. The wife is to give helpful but honest feedback when he wants it, and she should do it in a loving but serious manner. If you have nothing to say, don't respond for the sake of just giving an answer. The wife's feedback may not be accepted, but she should be clear and honest. Now, we are human, and there are times when the flesh gets in the way and wives may respond to their husbands' smart remarks in the same manner. Does it make it right? No, but it feels good. It takes practice to rebuke the devil at all times even when you are being disrespected by your husband, especially at the church. And it will happen. The challenge is to recognize that it is the work of the devil. Your husband may not see it that way, but for you, it is real. Although I did not handle it well, I learned that the right thing to do is to handle it at home behind closed doors. I am not saying to be a doormat. I don't believe God wants that either.

Remember to have respect for your husband even if his love for you is not shown at that time. Easier said than done, I know, but it is doable only with the help of the Holy Spirit.

Stand with your husband when things are tough, even when you disagree. Remember, he is human and has feelings. He is just a man who happens to be called by God. Pray him through it at all times while also praying for your strength in the situation. Know that the apostle Paul instructed all Christians to pray for one another, "with all prayer and supplication praying at all seasons in the Spirit, and watching thereunto in all perseverance and supplication for all the saints" Ephesians 6:18, which includes the wife praying for her husband. It's her responsibility and privilege to pray for her husband. It's good for him and the spiritual health of her home and life. They always say "happy wife, happy life." What about a happy husband who knows his wife has his back at all times? There should be a trust like none other for your man of God so he can be about God's business. You have his heart; don't abuse it. "The heart of her husband trusteth in her, And he shall have no lack of gain. She doeth him good and not evil All the days of her life" Proverbs 31:11–12. I came to believe that Satan desired to destroy my husband, especially his character and leadership in our relationship, sometimes using me as a pawn.

I came to understand that because I was his wife and younger than him, there were many times I was looked down upon. No matter what my spiritual walk was like, most assumed I did not have one or a relationship with Christ. There were many times I was dismissed as a nobody, and it seemed to be okay, meaning my pastor husband would not step in if I thought he should—not necessarily to come to my rescue but to demand church members respect me as his wife. That I still do not agree with, but it is how it was for me. So it can and will be lonely at times. Oh, but God!

It is said that preacher's kids are the worst. I disagree and would suggest that they are just ignored for the purpose of the ministry (the church and its members), and that can cause emotional turmoil for them. Pastors may not be doing this on purpose, but it is real for the children who go through it. Could that type of treatment be the reason they act out for attention outside the home? It's as if they think, *If I don't get it at home, I will get it from somewhere else, and then you have to pay attention to me.* That is why it is important for everyone (wife and children) to develop a relationship with Christ and determine where He wants him or her to serve in ministry. Now by no means does that excuse the pastor from making every attempt as father and husband to be there for his family, but his family's focus should be on serving God, which will keep the wife and children in line with the whole purpose of the family in the church. We cannot and should not act out, as we represent our head of the household and the church, the pastor, who is our husband and father. Not only that but we represent God, the Father, first.

Also understand that being ignored and left out is a part of being a member of the first family. It's nothing personal. Just do your part for the kingdom, which should be your main focus. Understand that the pastor is a man first. So he should do his part in paying attention to his family as well because when the church is gone, who is left there for him? His family? Right!

Thinking "if only" in retrospect does not help or improve a situation. Truth be told, if we knew what we were walking into, could we prepare better? I don't believe we could. There is not a proper handbook, and all the advice in the world from others, if you are lucky enough to get any, could prepare anybody for what was about to happen. Following are some of the situations that stand out for me and what I learned from them:

- Being who you are in Christ will never be enough. Everyone has his or her own perception of who you are to be. At times, it seemed as though I had to forget my life lessons and how I came to be who I was in Christ.

- You will be talked about no matter what you do or don't do.

- Some may think your ministry is fake or not valid or you do what you do just for attention or to be seen.

- There is always a stage! Every move is watched. Most of what you say will be taken the wrong way or not the way you intended it.

- Your feelings may not matter. It may seem you are not allowed to have any. Many cruel things were said to my face so I welcomed a tough skin.

- What you think or your opinion may not matter at all and sometimes not even to your husband.

- Being alone is the norm, although there are a few exceptions to this rule. It may seem that no one really wants to get close to you. However, be careful whom you trust. Sometimes there is a reason why a few want to be your friend. Again, there are several exceptions. There are genuine people who will show you they care about you and will be there for you.

I learned to lean on Colossians 3:23–24, "Whatsoever ye do, work heartily, as unto the Lord, and not unto men; knowing that from the Lord ye shall receive the recompense of the inheritance: ye serve the Lord Christ."

When we respond to the offer of salvation from Christ, we immediately accept a call to serve others and become Christ's presence in the world, using our gifts to bless His name, which then defines our purpose. In other words, find your purpose. "For we are his workmanship, created in Christ Jesus for good works, which God afore prepared that we should walk in them" (Ephesians 2:10). I had decided to create my own mission statement based on the gifts that God gave me and live by it.

Many won't or don't believe this about me, and that is okay because I am reminded that my Father put it in me for me. I would much rather be nameless and known for my ministry work than my name being known if I do not help or support God's people for His glory.

So what does it mean to be a first lady? Here are a few meanings I came to understand:

- It means that expectations of you will be like nothing you have ever experienced before in your walk with God.
- It means everyone will treat you differently and not always in a good way.
- It means that many will not try to get to know you but will base their opinion of you on what someone else said or thinks about you.
- It means allowing your feelings to be put on the back burner and showing grace under pressure.
- It means being ridiculed for just being who God made you to be.
- It means listening to negative and sometimes nasty comments about yourself and your family members, acting like you did not hear a thing, *and* sometimes having to explain it to your children to help them understand and get past it.
- It means watching what you say and whom you say it to.
- It means sharing your husband as the pastor at all times.
- It means living in a glass house and learning to block the stones thrown at it and being criticized even for doing that.
- It means being admired by some and not so much by others.

- It means what God gives you will be rejected at times. That does not mean you should not be obedient to it. There is always a way to bless His people.

- It means being lonely at times but not alone because God is always with you.

- It means your relationship with God will become so much more meaningful and make you stronger.

- It means not allowing your walk with God to change because you are just being tested.

- It means not complaining to your husband. Never let him see you sweat. Have a talk with Jesus.

- It means going in your secret closet for a good hard cry and coming out refreshed to start anew.

- It means God is preparing you for greater work in the kingdom for His glory.

- It means you will *never* be the same.

- I am in constant reminder mode now that I should never think higher of myself because many will put me on a pedestal. There should be respect but never disrespect for me or the role.

- I learned to minister to those God gives me and to concentrate on being my wonderfully made self in Christ Jesus, which will always be enough for Him.

Consider This

Do not allow any title to put you on a pedestal in your head. And being nameless or ignored is okay because with God your life and testimony make an impact for His glory.

STAGE 9

Ministry in Action
(Oh, but Not So Fast, New First Lady!)

Before I came to the church with my husband, I asked God, "What area of ministry should I pursue to bless Your people while giving You glory?" I would periodically check with Him on my spiritual gifts to see if I was in line with His will for my life and service. Let me say that spiritual gifts are there to show us what our purpose in life is, and it's important to know what they are so you understand how God can use you in His Service to bless His people and glorify Him—in other words, to understand why you do what you do.

At my other church homes, I was very active in service. I understood my gifts and used them in the Mission Society, Greeter's Ministry, and Dance Ministry and as the Young People's Department director. We served not only in the church but in the community, all over the state of Texas, and at conferences on a regular basis. We served and hosted quadrennials, welcoming people from other countries. We actively pursued the mission field. It was the norm for us to bless God's people, giving Him the glory along the way. We did not just talk about it. We were doers of the Word. I truly learned that we are called to strengthen our faith and sent to continue the ministry of Jesus Christ by service and witness to the world, and I chose to try to live it in my life. Doing so meant being a doer at church, at home, and in and around the community as well.

Growing up in the Baptist Church, I knew how it mainly operated as far as actually serving in missions. So looking back, I see that my coming in with a mind of active, continuous servanthood as first lady was not expected or accepted very well. And I knew that finding ways to stay motivated would be key and crucial to keeping my sanity. It would require continuous effort on my part so the focus wouldn't be on just being the first lady. I also understood that some would say, "You want to be seen because you choose to be busy about your Father's business" or doing what came naturally to me. That is par for the course and will happen no matter what you do. I would not become the church-lady pretending. I had to be okay if the church did not like who God made me to be. You might even run into those who think they are better than you in some way or holier than you, and that will have to be okay as well. Church folk will think what they will think. I found that suffering for Christ is a hard pill to swallow, but as my dear mother used to do, cut that pill up and drink a lot of water with it. That will make it go down easier. It became a way of blocking the demons sent to break me. There were those who were bold enough to voice it to my face, but my concern had to be on what God thought and said to me about me. Remember 1 Corinthians 13:4, 6, 8a: "Love suffereth long, and is kind; love envieth not; love vaunteth not itself, is not puffed up; rejoiceth not in unrighteousness, but rejoiceth with the truth; Love never faileth." That is the love of God. Again, your focus should be on being obedient to and pleasing God, who you know loves and accepts you and not on pleasing people. People will say they love you, but there may not be any action behind it. So for me, the question became would my husband as my pastor back me up with where God led me in ministry at the church? Would he love me through that? The challenge became being who God wanted me to be and at the same time trying to fit into what the church wanted me to be in the atmosphere they had already created. Understand that what the church thinks is not always what God wants for you and your ministry, and it will be questioned as if God did not give it to you. Soon after, I developed the mantra "What other people think about me is not my business." It can't be, and that is not being mean or facetious. That has to be between them and God. And I thought of a saying that Osho, an Indian spiritual teacher, once said, "Nobody is superior, nobody is inferior, but nobody is equal either. People are simply unique, incomparable. You are you, I am I." So the Holy Spirit had spoken yet again into my spirit for me to be me.

At my prior church, I was serving God as part of the dance ministry, which I had grown to love. There were times when I danced with God, and the world would stop, or so it seemed. God blessed me to start a community dance ministry with some young adult members of the new church, and we ministered all over Texas. That was a blessed time in the Lord! My honey pastor even asked me to birth a ministry at the church after my daughter and I ministered at one of the services. Working with those young people and watching them grow in service, giving back in ministry, blessed a lot of people. But the evil part of the world was still there lurking in the shadows, wanting turmoil and confusion to exist.

Over the years, dancing became something that caused all that to go away for a minute. The struggle of the flesh was always there, but God allowed an escape from it all. I learned that we never arrive at a point of no sufferings. The Bible says, "that ye may be sons of your Father who is in heaven: for he maketh his sun to rise on the evil and the good, and sendeth rain on the just and the unjust" Matthew 5:45. We must pay attention to how we go through the storm and whom we take with us, which will determine the outcome. The struggle is real. We can choose to come out broken or standing up ready to fight and continue in our Father's arms. The good news is that we always have a choice. God gives us that and is waiting on us to choose Him.

Know that if God leads you to minister in an unorthodox way or a way that is not the norm, you should be obedient and do what sayeth the Lord because if you are in His will, it will come out to please Him, even if only one person is blessed by it. I came to understand that God knows what He is doing. His Word says, "But he said, The things which are impossible with men are possible with God" Luke 18:27. And always remember that impossible is *I'm possible* when you break it down. So the way He gives you a ministry may seem crazy or impossible to others because it's not the way it was done in the past or what they are used to, but try not to let that discourage you. I had to remember to stay focused not on the journey but on the outcome, which is God's people getting blessed and being led to Christ. That is and always will be the main thing—that outcome, the outcome that glorifies the Father in heaven!

I learned that there are two motivations to serve, and they are your love for God and your love for His people. Staying focused means your service will become natural and you will be concerned about the needs of others and become compelled to help. My daughter used to ask me all the time why I always helped other people, especially those I did not know. It had become a way of life and still is for me. I used to tell her we are here to help others and that pleases God. It is not all about us. She being an only child had a problem with that concept, but she eventually learned it because of how we lived day to day. We are to "bear ye one another's burdens, and so fulfil the law of Christ. For if a man thinketh himself to be something when he is nothing, he deceiveth himself" Galatians 6: 2, 3. We are blessed to be a blessing to others. Period! It is not about us! When God blesses us with everything we need, we are not to hold on to it but share with those who really need help. First Peter 4: 9, 10 says, "Using hospitality one to another without murmuring: according as each hath received a gift, ministering it among yourselves, as good stewards of the manifold grace of God."

Obedience in service is a major key to giving God glory. My dominant gifts in the realm of service are helping and giving. Even if I wanted to, I could not stop myself from checking on people and seeing if they need support in some area. Visiting members and nonmembers alike was what we did on the regular. That foundation had been laid in us both before we became the pastor and wife of the church. God sent someone who was equally yoked in that area for me to serve with alongside in ministry. I was grateful for that area.

And as women, we can wear various hats. For me personally during the course of any week, I may have on any of the following: wife, mother, prayer warrior, cook, coworker, caregiver, nurse, volunteer, aunt, sister, cousin, niece, chauffeur, maid, counselor, friend, PTA board member, confidante, missionary, and last but not least, woman of God. There are times when these hats are stacked so high because we try to wear them all at the exact same time, but they won't all fit, and we begin to struggle and fail in many of the areas. That can lead to being overwhelmed and frustrated. Although we know that no one can multitask better than women, we have to learn that to alleviate frustration, we should just allow our top hat to be the crown worn as the daughter of the King. That way, everything else will fall into place as it should to honor the King, who was and is the best example of a true servant. Lesson learned! In the sixth chapter of Matthew verse 33, the Lord tells us to "seek ye first his kingdom, and his righteousness; and all these things shall be added unto you".

We think that success is determined by where we live or what we drive and even how busy we are. None of that is true. Success can be defined by how well you please God in your obedience in your service. Jesus's words in Matthew can prompt us to do a little hat reduction. Those we keep must be worn properly for any kind of success. Just remember to put the crown of being the daughter of the King in first place and listen to what He wants you to do for His service, which will help in placing your hats in their proper order. The late, great Muhammad Ali said it best: "Service is the rent we pay for a room here on earth." First lady or not, I choose to pay for my room.

Consider This

A servant of God is to be obedient to the will of God and His game plan whether others like it or not. One must learn to be okay with that concept and live in it.

STAGE 10

What Changed? (A Husband's Covering or a Pastor's Wife Left to Fend for Herself?)

I knew things would change, but no one could have prepared me for how drastic the change would become once I entered the church as a member. Wow! If only there was a basic how-to book for the pastor's wife that included age differences or any written information on that specific subject for that matter—just basic stuff because each person and church is different. Maybe that is why there is no handbook. Just maybe God wants us to truly try to figure out what it all means with His help. I did attend the National Baptist Convention class for pastors' and ministers' wives, but it did not cover my situation, and truth be told, there was nothing new. Just being his wife even before he becomes a pastor is not enough so-called training for the position because others are involved and the rules change. Whether you want to or not, you must adapt, or you will always be in your feelings and never do the service work that God intended for you to do. Yes, I said "position" earlier because unfortunately that is how it is treated and to many what it has become. Again, your feelings don't matter because it's not about you no matter how badly you are treated. Changing my way of thinking was challenging because at that time, I wanted my feelings to be acknowledged. I had to get out of me and into what was needed.

Change is hard because we get comfortable in our own lives and in doing things certain ways. So if it works, we think, *Why change?* but some lessons are there to make us better people, and if we look at it that way, change can be good. Remember to include God, and in time, His time, it will be better for all parties. However, the outcome of some changes can shake you to your core, and that is when you really have to rely on God to get you through. Remember, God is always there, especially during the times your husband is not because his focus is on the church. And if he is truly a man of God, God called him to be the pastor, and as his wife, you can't hold that against him. How you deal with the change is vital, but it becomes hard because you don't know how to maneuver through the newness of it all. The challenge is getting prepared for what is about to happen. How do you do that? I didn't know, and no one could tell me either. Now there were a lot of people in my ear, but discerning who was there to help or to hinder was another challenge in the beginning. So thank God for Jesus, who helped me with some of the following scenarios that I was not prepared for and did not understand.

I was not equipped to understand that just being myself was not good enough. I am an outgoing person who by nature can converse with everybody everywhere. So for me, not being prepared to handle being a pastor's wife with my personality was a shock. I did not realize that every conversation was being judged or graded in some way.

I was not ready to deal with so-called Christian criticism of my husband, my family, or myself. It was hard to deal with negative experiences, conflicts, and criticisms, especially in relation to my husband and our area of ministry, which was service. I would at times feel resentment when it came to the church and sometimes to my honey pastor because I thought he could have handled some things differently when it came to us. So, yes, there were times when I was not very pleasant or seemed hard to some. And I had to be reminded and keep in mind Psalm 105:15: "Saying, Touch not mine anointed ones, And do my prophets no harm." I was doing harm to my husband, and that was wrong. How dare I do what some others were doing to him? God had to help me with that spirit.

I was not prepared when the church seemed to forget that my husband was human. My understanding was to respect people and reverence God. Okay, so I understood that to respect someone, such as a pastor, is to admire him or her based on a quality or ability. And to reverence is to fear and fall down before or be in awe of someone who is superior, such as God or the Holy Spirit. So for me, at times, those roles seemed to be reversed by many, and the lines got blurred. Those blurred lines can bring the author of confusion into the atmosphere.

It took me totally by surprise to feel unprotected by my husband—not the pastor but my husband. I wish someone had told me that my husband could not be God for me at the church, meaning that he as a prior pastor for many years and of a certain age would not protect me from what I had stepped into. I learned that I should not make my problems or how I was being treated his problem. It was the hardest thing for me to do because one should be able to share one's experiences of hurt with one's spouse, or so I thought. But I was disillusioned at first to find out that he indeed had the issues of the whole church to deal with constantly, which made no time for me, his wife. This is how I learned to separate the pastor from my husband and take it to God.

I was not equipped for everything we did or didn't do to be watched (the glass house syndrome as it has been called). Even though we both were being watched, learning not to allow myself to be controlled by the expectations of that was a hard thing to do. This is still a challenge for me as the wife of a pastor. Oh, but God reminds me that it's not really about me or us but what others want us to be in their eyes. So that glass house can be broken with the change of our mindset. It's in how I choose to accept or not accept that expectation.

It caught me by surprise at how some mean and really disrespectful people were okay with being that way and showing it. I had to learn not to pay too much attention to negative Nellies by praying for myself first and then for them as well, or they would get me down. I also had to learn to watch what I said and to whom I said it. Most times, it would be repeated and changed from what or how I said it. I had to remind myself it was out there and to let it go and remember that I was going home with him. I would try not to bring it home.

In my case, I was not equipped to handle how much my husband did not need or use me. His being older could have been the reason for this because our situation was new for him as well. Also, this was his second church, and he was so proud to be used in that way again. I had to keep reminding myself of those facts and that it was not about me because I really didn't know if he even knew how to use me. However, this was very, very hard for me, as I was used to working and being involved in the service to God's people in the church. I also thought we would work in ministry as a couple literally because that was one of the things that attracted him to me, my work in the church. He would verbalize that often. I found out that dealing with God's people, some of whom were very critical, in the church was difficult enough, and I realized that he seemed not to know how to incorporate me into ministry as a partner, so to speak. So was I wrong in thinking it was because of my age? Case in point, in just trying to plan an event with the leadership for the new pastor and wife, I was rejected.

I am not sure why. That was hard to swallow because he okayed it, and we spent money to prepare. It was designed to fellowship, a chance to get to know one another and say we were glad we were there and excited to work in ministry with them. It was a chance for him to begin to share what God gave him for leadership at the church and formally introduce me. That was it! But lesson learned. I was made to feel that only at home and on pastoral care visits (he and I alone) could I cheer him on and show how much he made a difference in the lives of God's people. Those were the best times! And more important, that was the time for me to work the ministry that God had placed into me.

Other times, I had to learn that I would be secondary and sometimes disrespected. And by the way, know that more times than not, whatever you do for him in his ministry may go unnoticed or the credit may be given to someone else—not that you want credit but some acknowledgment from your husband as pastor of what God gave you to share with him and the church would go a long way. Let's be real. It matters because we are human and having our contributions acknowledged by our husband pastor would be nice, to say the least. That was when I really learned to allow him to come to me for help if he needed me. Just understand that your husband will be very busy, and there may seem to be no time for you. Expect that. But you should go alongside him in the areas of time management, organization, and service to God's people when allowed.

I wish someone had told me that being obedient to God and actively doing ministry for His glory would become a struggle in the church. I found that is when the devil becomes really busy because he wants to stop God's program from going forth. I kind of knew that concept but had not actually experienced it in a large area like the church. I had to keep remembering that I was entering a unique situation, an established church membership, although the church was no more than a few members who were attempting to start over, which was a new journey for them as well, and ministry was not on the forefront of the agenda. There were auxiliaries (providing supplementary or additional help and support) inside the church and not ministries (the spiritual work or service of any Christian or a group of Christians) outside the church, which I was used to being involved in. So now the author of division was showing up to cause havoc.

God has always shown me ways to bless His people in one way or another. Being active was my norm, but there were those who did not think the first lady should be as active as I was. I had to keep reminding myself that favor in doing active ministry is not fair. Someone will always have something to say, whether good or bad. Oh, but God in His majesty gave me a way out as I continued to be obedient to His call in other areas outside the church and as a continued lifestyle.

Again, focus on the outcome and not the journey. It does not matter how you get there because you might get some scars and bruises along the way, but wear those with honor and realize they were from lessons learned. Sometimes sweating the small stuff makes the situation a lot worse than it has to be. As long as the people are blessed and God is glorified, it will be worth it. I learned that if God gave me something to do for His kingdom, He would supply what was needed and a way to get it done. So I chose not to be "religious" but effective for His sake! Just be obedient whether you are protected by your honey pastor or not. Hallelujah!

Consider This

Try remembering that no one can prepare you for the ups and downs of any relationship. There is no exact handbook available for each situation. Change will come. A husband can protect (he has to choose to), *but* only God can cover, which will always be enough.

STAGE 11

Staying Focused on God's Will for Us with His Help (Servants for God or Serving Others' Expectations?)

When God blesses you with a second chance at anything, trust and be mindful of how you handle it, especially a relationship. It can be hard not to compare it to past relationships, but you should make a sincere effort not to do that. We both had been single for many years. However, we knew what would not work for us because of those experiences from our past. Even though we were married to different people, we had experienced some of the same situations. We had to be mindful not to allow the devil a way in and understand that mistakes are our best teachers. Therefore, taking serious note of any past mistakes would help in going forth in this new relationship. Mistakes are there for us to learn ways of doing things differently or the right way, God's way. Yes, we messed up and probably will again, but we had to forgive ourselves and not dwell on it. We had to move forward. "But one thing I do, forgetting the things which are behind, and stretching forward to the things which are before. I press on toward the goal unto the prize of the high calling of God in Christ Jesus" Philippians 3:13b, 14. Lesson learned: let go, and let God!

Now the focus had to be on giving the new relationship a chance to honor what God had put together. God had to be in the forefront of this whole situation, at home for the marriage and at church, or we knew it would not work. Wisdom comes through strife and turmoil. One just has to acknowledge it and use it. One way to do that is to begin to worship God. Putting focus on Him in your situation will allow it to work or prosper because your heart and mind or conscience will be clear to move in it and from it. Get the lesson because that is your wisdom kicking in to change you for the better.

We knew that some change would be inevitable whether we welcomed it or not. It will happen in some form or fashion. However, our core values, if we really believe in them, should never change because we not only believe them but we make an active attempt to live them. They make up our character and show who we choose to be—again, *choose* to be, not who people think we are or who they want us to be. I saw this in action in my honey pastor time and time again. God had truly transformed this man from how he was in his younger days. The stories he would tell me of his foolish shenanigans from his past were hard to believe, but it showed just how God can take a mess and make it a blessing for His glory. From some of the things he had done, he should truly be in a grave no doubt. His mantra back in the day when he arrived at a party was "The devil can go home because Coleman is in the house!"

Oh, but God had a different plan for his life, as He stepped in and made a dramatic change in him. His grace was sufficient! His life story would definitely be a number-one best seller. We discussed it many times, but God did not lead him to put pen to paper as he did for me. I had to accept that, but it would have blessed so many to know just how God cleaned him up for His service. God has allowed him to share some of his testimony on several occasions. At any rate, it had to be his strong belief in God that allowed him to be emotionally mistreated and disrespected by others. Yes, we understand that comes with the title of pastor. He often chose not to say or do anything about it. Being humble and taking the high road in many degrading situations is what he was so good at doing, or so I thought, but it was God in him in action. That was growth in the wisdom of God in his life. I truly admired so many things about him as a man of God, and that was one of them. That showed true maturity in Christ and that he knew who he was in Christ. He was so good at knowing when to walk away from situations. It allowed others and me to see what kind of man he truly was. He used to say that your life should be your sermon. Live what you teach and preach about. That is the best way to honor God. He is who you want to please. He would say the Bible says this or that. Always go to God and ask Him to "Teach me to do thy will; For thou art my God: Thy Spirit is good; Lead me in the land of uprightness" Psalm 143:10. It was evident that his focus was on God.

He was called back into full-time ministry as the pastor in the fifth year of our marriage. When this happened, I asked him, "What do you want my role to be at the church, if any?" This was a new journey we were about to take together, so we needed to talk about how this would play out. He had been in the pastor's role before, but I had never been the pastor's wife or first lady. There was never a real answer to my question about what he wanted my role to be in the church. He only said, "Continue to do what you have been doing." So I was thinking that I came from a church where the ministry of actively serving God's people was constant, and he knew that because he saw me actively serving all the time in and outside the church when he visited my church, and he said he loved that about me. So how would that translate to our new church home?

We knew churches were different in how they operated. There are certain traditions done here and not there, right? I still wanted and needed to know how this would translate from AME mode to Baptist mode with him as the pastor. With no specific answer, I thought, *Okay, God, You will have to take the wheel and drive for sure with this one. Please lead and guide us both and continue to allow my service to be for You alone and not others' expectations.*

Life is hard enough without everyone in your business. Why do some church folk believe that they belong smack-dab in the middle of your life just because he is the pastor? Where in the Bible does it say that the pastor's household should be an open book for the church and membership to participate in, dictate to, and make decisions for? Knowing the character of the pastor and assisting him at the church is one thing, but trying to run his household is another. The Bible says for the church to take care of the pastor. First Timothy 5:17 says, "Let the elders that rule well be counted worthy of double honor, especially those who labor in the word and in teaching." It also says that the man (no matter his vocation, not mentioned) should take care of his family because the man is the head. "And Jehovah God took the man, and put him into the garden of Eden to dress it and to keep it; And Jehovah God said, It is not good that the man should be alone; I will make him a help meet for him" Genesis 2:15, 18. Yet again let's be clear about what the Bible says. In Genesis 1:26, it says that God said "Let's create man" (some versions say human beings) in His own image, or likeness. And verses 27 and 28 say,

> And God created man in his own image, in the image of God created he him;
> male and female created he them. And God blessed them: and God said unto

them, Be fruitful, and multiply, and replenish the earth, and subdue it; and have dominion over ... every living thing that moveth upon the earth.

So that old adage saying that if the pastor takes care of the church, God will take care of the family is not a completely true statement. He has a responsibility to take care of his family too, which includes his wife. Again, it cannot be stressed enough that this should be a couple thang. Hence the word *them*!

We see all the time that double honor is mostly thought of as just finances—wages and allowances in the church. Maybe that is the reason some may think *Since we are paying you, we can treat you any way we wish whether according to God's* Word *or not.* What about respect for the person God called to pastor the people? What about showing that respect in allowing him to see the change in you, the members, from his teaching and preaching the Word of God so what he does is not in vain? What about him living his sermons for all to see as the example of what he teaches and preaches? What about truly seeing his character and allowing him to take care of his household? What about appreciation and respect for his family members who give in various ways alongside him in his service to the church? Why is that not enough?

Consider This

Serving the church for God should not hurt the flesh of the man (the pastor) or woman (the first lady) of God, nor their family. Remember, meeting God's expectations will never hurt you but those of humankind sometimes will.

STAGE 12

Family Time without the Church is a Must-Have

I have found that when you focus on yourself and your stuff with your family, you have less stress. Now don't get me wrong; dealing with family can be just as stressful as dealing with others, but when others are not in your stuff, it seems easier to navigate. God gives a different kind of peace when that happens. Maybe that is because the expectations are different or not as high because you know the involved people better than outsiders.

Let's think about the family unit for a minute. What did God really intend for it to be? Well, He did put man and woman together as one, and part of their mandate was to be fruitful and multiply, right? Knowing that, for me, unity comes to mind when I think about family. If you do not have each other's back as a family, you can bet there will be much turmoil outside the home, whether you are the first family or not. That unity has to be intentional in action and not just for appearances. Yes, there will be times when even though you love each other, you won't like each other. Those times come when the pastor seems to push the family aside for the church more times than not. You have to work through that just like anything else.

A good support system is when one truly cares about family members and makes a commitment that they will come first with God no matter what comes their way. Let's not forget when the church is gone, family will still be there. Feeling that support from each other means more than words can say.

We had that at home, but at the church, it seemed to change because the church came first. We must understand that the order of God, family, career or vocation, and then everything else should be our practice. Also, having God first is not having the church first. *That should be repeated: putting God first is not the same thing as putting the church first!* God and the church are not one and the same as a lot of people, including pastors, treat them. For me, therein lies the issue of the family being ignored or put on the back burner. Truth be told, the church is treated like a business at times and a pastor is a vocation because they pay him, so should the church be included in the "career section" or the "everything else" section I spoke about before? We seem to get this twisted.

Understand that each individual in a family should have God first—not just the pastor. Each member of the family should have his or her own personal relationship with God before anything else. Everything in perspective makes a difference. The pastor must make time for family and family only, just as he makes time for the church. Family with God should be the backbone from which everything else springs into action. We understand that the man of God needs to get rest and should be refreshed, renewed, and revived in his walk as well. I understood that some of that responsibility lay on the wife in being the helpmeet God intended. The wife knows that he must be able to give to God's people on the daily, but how can he if he is never filled up himself? My honey pastor used to say all the time that home should be a piece of heaven here on earth. That concept has to be created and cultivated consistently by all members of the family, including the pastor or husband as the head of the family. That is the wife taking care of the home and the children obeying their parents too. We tend to forget that everyone has a part to play for the sake of the family being successful in God's eyes, doing it His way. That will bring on harmony to make the home become a piece of heaven on earth.

I am grateful that knowing he married a woman with a young child, he would think of ways to do things as a family. He wanted my daughter to have family experiences as a youngster and would put effort into making it happen. So he was involved in her school projects and went to some events at church and school functions she participated in. He made sure she had all supplies needed for whatever. He was big on traveling, so we took family trips. We attended church conventions and family reunions. And the nice thing about it all was that he as the pastor left the church behind during those vacations. He actually took time away from it all, which impressed me because I know sometimes it can't be turned off. His actions away showed what he talked about or said he would do. That was refreshing in a man, and I believe that because he was older and knew who he was, it made it possible for him to be that way. The essential building block of humanity is the family. It's God's plan for the ages. Let's remember that all involved should make a conscious effort to make it matter.

Consider This

Make a concerted effort to do your part to make the family what God intended it to be. To have every person contributing to the same cause, the family, now that would be pleasing to a loving God!

STAGE 13

When the Pulpit is behind the Pastor

A few years ago, I was walking by the television, and a reporter was interviewing an elderly gentleman who was celebrating his birthday. I forget exactly how old he was, but it was one hundred and something. He asked him about his secret of longevity, and his answer was three things that I believe should be considered by all: one, stop eating when you are still hungry; two, wake up (stop sleeping) when you are still tired; and three, stop talking when you still have something to say. They sound so simple, but if you think about it, they are very hard to do because they require a tremendous amount of self-control. They all require one to stop. That is the operative word in all three things.

I was pleasantly surprised when the conversation of retiring from the church came up, and he actually did not want to stay in the pulpit forever. At some point, he realized he had to stop. And he welcomed it. Only you and your willpower or desire with a made-up mind can do that, right? Well, when your willpower or desire is gone or taken away, then what? When you become a certain age and have no more fight because of situations beyond your control, then what? If that is your husband going through that, how do you cope as a wife—first lady or not? You have to develop your own strategy for the struggle. Because what happens when the elders of the church stop calling to pray over or even with you? What happens when the church is silent, when there are secret meetings that you are not invited to? What happens when members have claimed they love you, but there is no evidence behind it now that you are not in the pulpit? I now understand that the love and respect is for the position and not the person who gives so much of himself to it, sometimes choosing to stay on until death.

We know God allows things to happen to see how we will react to the situation, to see if we turn to Him if left alone. He knows as a pastor's wife I do that often, but what will the pastor do? One would think that this would be one of those times when the pastor would begin to live even more in those things he preached about to many congregations, right? But what happens when you are abruptly blindsided with the reality that you are no longer wanted or needed? Will you depend only on God for help—that help being love, guidance, comfort, direction, or healing? Will there be someone of the flesh other than the first lady to help you in your time of need or confusion, whether it be to nurse you back to health, run errands, get you food, or even help you transition? Is that not what we, as the pastor and wife, did and continue do for the church and its membership? Now I am speaking on portions of my life that I lived through. Please remember that these are my experiences.

I know I will get talked about for speaking my mind on my experiences. Some will say that I am just complaining and that something is wrong with me for having these feelings and they are not justified. Oh, the conversations that will be held after this book comes out and how the stage will never be the same again! Been there, done that! It will be a new chapter that I can handle because I know whose I am and He is with me through it all, lesson learned! Oh, and please understand what I know is that a gracious, forever-loving

God has led me in this walk to get through all the aforementioned and more. Therefore, I will continue to do what He leads me to do for His glory! The saying "If He brings you to it, He will bring you through it" is so true. I dealt with it before becoming the pastor's wife, so it was not new to me in that role. When you try to live for God and do what He tells you to do, the devil will show up. Does it hurt? Yes, but your service to God's people for His glory must continue on. And know that God will send those He wants you to bless. Remember, it is always about pleasing Him, walking in the favor He gives you. There was my aunt with cancer, church members in the hospital, nursing home residents who had no one, my uncle with heart disease, and even my beloved mother, who suffered many strokes, which lead to the dreaded Alzheimer's disease, and, yes, even now, my honey pastor, who survived a mild heart attack and stroke at the same time. Caring for others can be grueling, but it can also be rewarding because it is of God. Just like anything else, it is all in your perspective on the situation. Is it pleasing to God when you are helping others? What about just being there for someone, which will make a big difference in his or her life? To honor God we must honor His people by showing them we care. There is an action again.

I would rather be nameless and known for my ministry work than my name being known if I do not help or support God's people and His program. Taking care of others or God's people should be the norm.

> Is any among you sick? let him call for the elders of the church; and let them pray over him, anointing him with oil in the name of the Lord: And the prayer of faith shall save the *sick*, and the Lord shall raise him up; and if he have committed sins, they shall be forgiven him. Confess your faults one

to another, and pray one for another, that ye may be healed. The effectual

fervent prayer of a righteous man availeth much. James 5:14–16

Does that not apply to your pastor, even if his wife is the one calling the elders of the church? Our situation could be considered unique, but we knew and served a good God, who allowed all this to manifest for our good. Only we did not see or expect it. Just as we had composed a letter of resignation to present to the church, the deacons decided out of the blue to retire him as pastor with the title pastor emeritus. So the letter was never presented to the church. And it was not really out of the blue, as a plan was clearly in place and had been thought out very carefully, which was revealed later as time went by, but no one told the pastor. The fact is the way it was done did not seem Godly to us or to many others, including members. But as he graciously told the church, the last time he was permitted to speak to them, "I don't understand it, but God's got it." And so it was.

The next week, the church packed up his stuff, put him out of the pastor's office, shoved his belongings into a much smaller office, and removed his name from the sign in front of the church—nothing Christlike about it. Who knew what was around the corner for us? Only God knew, and we had to lean on Him for this new chapter in our lives. That was what we did. What he began to go through next was difficult to watch as his wife because it started a ripple effect of life changes, and a lot of emotions took over in a very short period of time. Only one other time in my life did I feel so helpless—when my child was very sick, and we ended up at the hospital alone. So being alone came into play again because he shut me out.

I am a problem solver, but I knew I could not solve this and it was not my place to fix it, but not even being able to comfort my husband was devastating to say the least. There was no discussion about what happened or how he felt about it, but a wife can see and feel the emotions as time goes on. So here is where my strategy for my struggle strongly came into being. First, there was total disbelief because it was unexpected. No one called or came over to have a conversation about anything. Imagine that: on one Wednesday night, you are called into the office and told that this is what will happen, and the very next week, on Wednesday night, it will be announced to the church, not even on Sunday so the whole congregation can be involved in the vote. Having God in you, as my husband did, you go along to get along, which he was known to do.

Second, there is confusion because now you are being ignored like you were never there. And there are so many unsolicited reports from nonmembers, some in other cities, and reliable sources, stating that they knew about it and thought it would happen while the church was in its very early stages and original building. Let's not forget that under his leadership, land was purchased and a new edifice was built and completed. So we remember that if the Lord is for you, who in the world can be against you? His work will go forth even in the midst of foolishness by humankind. Again, there is a lesson in it all for us. Praise God! That building was and is for God's people and for the good of the kingdom, right? But being honest, in the flesh, how can you not think that it was all planned, and you were used for your name and reputation only? And now you are there in the pulpit and being chastised at times or ignored to send a message that you are no longer the pastor. After a while, it can wear on you, whether you admit it or not. And he, my honey pastor, never complained or talked about it. Remember, I as the wife was living through this with him as well.

Third, the spirit of brokenness came to visit, which led to a deep depression that it seemed no one cared about or believed was real. There were comments about his being contrary or stubborn or even angry at the church, which was not true, but no one who was under his leadership in the beginning bothered to come see what the actual truth was. We know it is easy for people, especially church folks, to create a narrative about what they think is going on with others, which becomes their truth. What is worse is when that same narrative is spread around, and then others are repeating that untruth. Now I must say there was one minister who did come and check on my husband periodically after this happened, and we were so grateful—me especially as his wife because there was a noticeable change after those visits. However, depression is real, and it does harm and is not nice. What can a wife do with that spirit of depression when the hold becomes tighter and tighter and the person with it has lost all zeal for life? Psalm 18:14 says, "The spirit of a man will sustain his infirmity; But a broken spirit who can bear?"

Having a will to live can help one fight off sickness, but a broken spirit? No one lives well with that. So when the church no longer wants you and your heart is the church, how do you cope? What do you do when it seems as though God is not present in your situation? Your thought pattern becomes *Where is He?* So again, how does one cope? That is the million-dollar question. Again, I ask, when it seems that God, whom you turn to for help in all situations is silent, what do you do? The only other alternative would be to turn to people, whom you probably started out with, so now what? We all know that people will let us down. But God said He would never leave us or forsake us, so He has been and is there all along. He knows all about the situation, so what does that silence look like? What exactly does it mean, and how do you figure it out without going crazy? It would be easy to allow your emotions to get the better of you when you don't hear from God, but is that what He would want? That was the next big question that God had to answer for the pastor and me. I had to come to the realization that I could only do so much in our new situation.

God also reminded me that all of us were in new territory. A good pastor had not been removed before, so maybe we were all just doing the best we could do. It's possible, but when underhanded things are done and no one admits accountability, that is not of God and that is what hurts and makes it hard to digest. So you accept and move out of the way. That is what my husband did, and he still got chastised for it. Yes, with him being older, I was prepared to take care of him in his golden years. That is what spouses do, and I am a caregiver at heart. Remember, I had done that before with relatives and church members. We understand that in this day and age, people are living longer, and many have full lives if they do what's needed to sustain them. He has one of the best doctors who treats him as if he is his own father. Together, they got him to the age of sixty-seven, which was when we first met. At that time, he looked much younger, and no one could believe his age because of it. That was another reason age was not an issue for us: he took such pride in taking care of himself. He would walk at the park regularly for exercise and take his meds faithfully. His thinking was that if God did His part, he would do his to keep healthy in order to serve God's people. He actually promised me thirty years of life together. So again, I ask what happens when that way of thinking is gone or taken away because of circumstances beyond your control, and it seems as though he does not care about truly being active in living for himself, let alone for God, and just exists?

Lastly, the spirit of dementia came for a visit, and it is staying way past its unwelcome time. But let's be real. If you factor in age, a few health issues due to age, and an earlier lifestyle that was not really good for you because of what you put into your body, the mind will begin to settle and slow down, right? We understand that God did not design us to be here on the earth forever. In order to be with Him in paradise, we must leave here at some point. However, to watch someone slowly deteriorate is very hard to do. Honestly, that is what happens when one is left to feel one is no longer needed or wanted, which is what I see when I visit nursing facilities. Now it was up close and personal because it was in our home. No matter how many times you have seen it happen and lived through it, family or not, it is still hard. The progression of life the way God intended is real, and it will happen the way He intended it to happen no matter what, whether we want it to happen that way or not. Moving our feelings out of it is the challenge we face. God knows that, so you would think that keeping the situation before Him would make it easier to handle, right? Well, no, because we tend to stay in the flesh when times are hard or not going the way we want, and that can make it even harder. We become our own worst enemy when we don't get out of our own way and allow God to handle our problems.

Again, we must find the lesson in it all. God is speaking to us through all the misery that comes. James 1:2 says, "Count it all joy, my brethren, when ye fall into manifold temptations." Temptations are there to make us want to do and or feel a certain way that is mostly not good. They can bring on misery, but we can choose not to accept it by not listening or buying into it and worshipping God through it. Fighting to listen is one of the most challenging things one will ever do, but that fight with the help of the Holy Spirit can be won. Oh, and the God I serve is there because He cares for us! That is how we can find that joy.

One of my favorite scriptures says, "Casting all your anxiety upon him, because he careth for you". 1 Peter 5:7. Another one is Proverbs 18:10, which says, "The name of Jehovah is a strong tower; The righteous runneth into it, and is safe." In His hands, I have to believe it will be all right because He cares, and we are safe.

Consider This

Misery will come and can be an option unless you become ill and don't even realize that you are miserable. An all-knowing God is still in the midst and always a better option, so lean on Him.

STAGE 14

Calmness is Here because God's Got Us in and through It All

My husband is living proof of God's amazing grace on an individual's life. He, with his humble spirit, has shown that when your actions are not of God, God indeed can change them. And whatever was done to him God was blocking it—we see that now—God was not through with him and allowed him to go many places and bless a lot of His people. I was privileged to be a part of many of those blessings. God used him, and because of that, I can see he is at peace. God showed me that I had to come to terms with him now being different, and his time in actual service would be also. He had given all he could give, and it was time to rest. Another lesson learned but a hard one for me since I was and still am in my prime. Nevertheless, I get it now.

There is nothing like peace on people when they realize they are in line with fulfilling their God-given purpose. Even though my husband no longer moves like he used to, he is at peace. Even though he can't think like he used to, he is at peace. Even though he has trouble remembering some of his former life or certain people, he is at peace. The circle of life is real and just as God planned it.

We come into this world as babies, innocent and unknowing. We learn, grow, and prayerfully attempt to live a life worthy of the grace and mercy God gives us as His beloved children. We make mistakes, but we grow by getting valuable lessons from those mistakes. We also understand that some of the stuff we learn is not for our good so we have to unlearn some things as we grow in wisdom.

As for me, that strategy for struggle I spoke about earlier is to remember and rely on these few tidbits I learned along the way: I know that I am never alone; that nothing takes God by surprise—He knew I would be where I am today; that when I am weak, He is strong, so I must learn to always lean on Him for my strength; that He is the God of new beginnings, but that new beginning may not look like I think it should; and that His love never ever gives up on me, so I won't ever give up on Him and turn away. I also realized that my honey pastor did not turn his back on God; he just lost sight of himself for a moment. And in that space of time, he had nothing to give to God. Transitioning from being independent to being dependent is hard for anyone and takes time to adjust to. Some never adjust. It was all new to him, and he did not like it at all, which was understandable. I saw his struggle in trying to be his own man, continuing to make his decisions and keep his wits about him as he knew them. In times of making adjustments like these in life, it can seem unbearable on both the pastor going through the transition and his wife, his caregiver. There needs to be time to adjust to a new normal. That is a time when one really has to use spiritual gifts like patience and compassion and much prayer to make it through.

Having to accept that we will have battles to fight and we may want to abandon our identities or our values because of the stress of it all is more challenging when the mind begins to deteriorate because of illness. But let's always remember that the Word says, "My flesh and my heart faileth; But God is the strength of my heart and my portion for ever". Psalm 73:26

I leave you with some of what I know for certain and what I consider lessons learned over the years. Your value does not decrease because others refuse to see your worth. God created you, so that proves you are worthy of life. He wants you to nurture that life and honor Him in all you do with His creation that is you. Remember, nothing is about you or your spouse. Everything is about God the Father. Focus on Him and truly understand what He will do in your life first and then in your marriage. Never stop working on yourself as an individual so you can contribute to your marriage in a healthy way. It takes two fleshly beings and one spiritual being in any relationship. We must allow God to guide above *any and all* circumstances. 1 Kings 22:5

I have come to consider no matter what I am going through these three things are true: God is there with me, God is using me in some way to help others and teach me a lesson, and it won't always last, whatever it is. Again, I will never forget one of the last things that my honey pastor said when he spoke to the church body the night they announced he was being retired. He said, "God's got us!"

Even in the midst of me taking care of him on a daily basis, those words ring true. Our normal is different. Our communication is different. It can be a struggle, but it is where we are, and God is here in the midst. I now also understand that suffering for God is not of human will.

Staying in His will makes it tolerable, and trusting those around who sincerely want to help or support is hard but necessary in order to trust God and what He is doing in the midst of it all. Sharing and writing this memoir has helped me get those points of clarity on where I am in my life. It is not meant to hurt anyone in any kind of way. It is just my truth as I see and live it. I realize some will not agree, and again, I will be looked at differently. So be it. God is with me, and calm is here.

Has my marriage been a fairy tale? No. Did I have all the strength I needed to be a first lady? No. That task was much larger than I was. I tried to be a devoted wife, mother, and friend who was mission-inspired in helping others along the way. Is my living in vain? No, because I will press on toward the mark of a higher calling, living as my Father God sees fit and allowing Him to order my steps.

So I now know that a loving God always has my back, front, sides, top, and bottom. And as my favorite song says, "Because He lives, I can face tomorrow." I am so grateful!

And so the stages continue—but my walk on the stage is different because now I am wiser. I am still flawed but different, always leaning on my Daddy, God, in all situations. Bless my heart!

Consider This

No matter what, I remember my first line of defense is to look to God for help. He is always there with open arms, willing and waiting on me to come to Him for guidance. *God, U & I Dance!*

I leave you with this edited version of an old fable from Aesop, just food for thought …

The Story of the Old Man, a Boy, and a Donkey

An old man, a boy, and a donkey were going to town. The boy rode on the donkey, and the old man walked beside him. As they went along, they passed some people who remarked it was a shame the old man was walking and the boy was riding. The man and boy thought maybe the critics were right, so they changed positions.

Later, they passed some people who remarked, "What a shame! He makes that little boy walk." They then decided they would both walk.

Soon they passed some more people who thought they were stupid to walk when they had a decent donkey to ride. So they both rode the donkey.

Now they passed some people who shamed them by saying how awful it was to put such a load on a poor donkey. The boy and man said they were probably right, so they decided to carry the donkey.

As they crossed the bridge, they lost their grip on the animal, and he fell into the river and drowned.

The moral of the story is if you try to please everyone, you might as well kiss your own ass goodbye.

Consider This

Be you because everybody else is taken, and ask yourself, "Will God bless who I pretend to be?"

SPECIAL ACKNOWLEDGMENTS

(I know trouble will come by calling names, but guess what—with God, I can handle it. Amen!)

To our dear friend (*you know who you are*), who really started it all by introducing us and who told each of us in private individually not to hurt the other, thank you for allowing God to use you to see what could be and for continuing to stand with us! We truly love you!

To other true, die-hard sister friends in Christ and whatever else I need them for—AH, CS, BP, RJ, CW, DH, TH, and ET (RIH!)—none of you have changed from day one of our first meeting once I stepped on this stage. Thanks for hanging in by listening, encouraging, chastising, and praying with your girl in the good, bad, and ugly of it all! Your support for me on this stage means more than you will ever know. I thank God for each of you and pray for your well-being and success!

And last but most definitely not least, in remembrance of my beloved momma, Mrs. Dee Esther Crowe Jones. Oh, how you are missed! I realize you were not on board at first, but God worked that out too. I know you are watching, and I pray I am making you proud. You were literally the hardest-working woman I have ever known. I am at peace in knowing that in some way, I did all I could do to make your life better as your baby daughter. Thank you for *all* you did for me on this side of heaven and for cherished memories of lessons left behind. You were appreciated, and I apologize for the times I did not say or show it! I know it was hard for you, but you did the best you could do. For that, I love you and always will. Continue to rest in our Savoir!

> There hath no temptation taken you but such as man can bear: but God is faithful, who will not suffer you to be tempted above that ye are able; but will with the temptation make also the way of escape, that ye may be able to endure it.
>
> —1 Corinthians 10:13

Find your escape in the loving arms of God and stay there in order to get through. Thrive in your survival.

INSPIRATIONAL RESOURCES

Aesop. "The Old Man, a Boy, and a Donkey." Original Fable. *Aesop's Fables.* (Google edited version). Greece: 1867

Cameron, Micah. Artist Front Cover Artwork

https://en.wikipedia.org/wiki/Lucy_Webb_Hayes Lucy Webb Hayes from Wikipedia, the free encyclopedia

Holmes, Duana. Author Photo

Lawsen, Carolyn. *God Moments for Women.* IL: Christian Arts Gifts, 2012.

https://www.nps.gov › travel › presidents › first_ladies_nhs First Ladies National Historic Site Ohio

St. John-Gilbert, Rachel. *Wake Up Laughing.* Uhrichsville, OH: Barbour Publishing, 2011.

https://www.usatoday.com/story/sports/boxing/2016/06/03/muhammad-ali-best-quotes-boxing/85370850/.

https://www.whitehouse.gov › about-the-white-house › first-ladies Harriet Land / The White House The biographies of the First Ladies on WhiteHouse.gov are from "The First Ladies of the United States of America," by Allida Black. Copyright 2009 by the White House Historical Association.

https://www.whitehousehistory.org/the-origins-of-the-american-first-lady The Origins of the American "First Lady" by Matthew Costello, Vice President of the Rubenstein Center for White House History, Senior Historian

Also by Author, written for Young Adults

Mistakes Don't Have to Stay

One Day or Day One, We can Decide

Lessons Learned through God's Grace

Experienced by Amy J Lee-Coleman